ESMÉ THOMPSON

THE ALCHEMY OF DESIGN

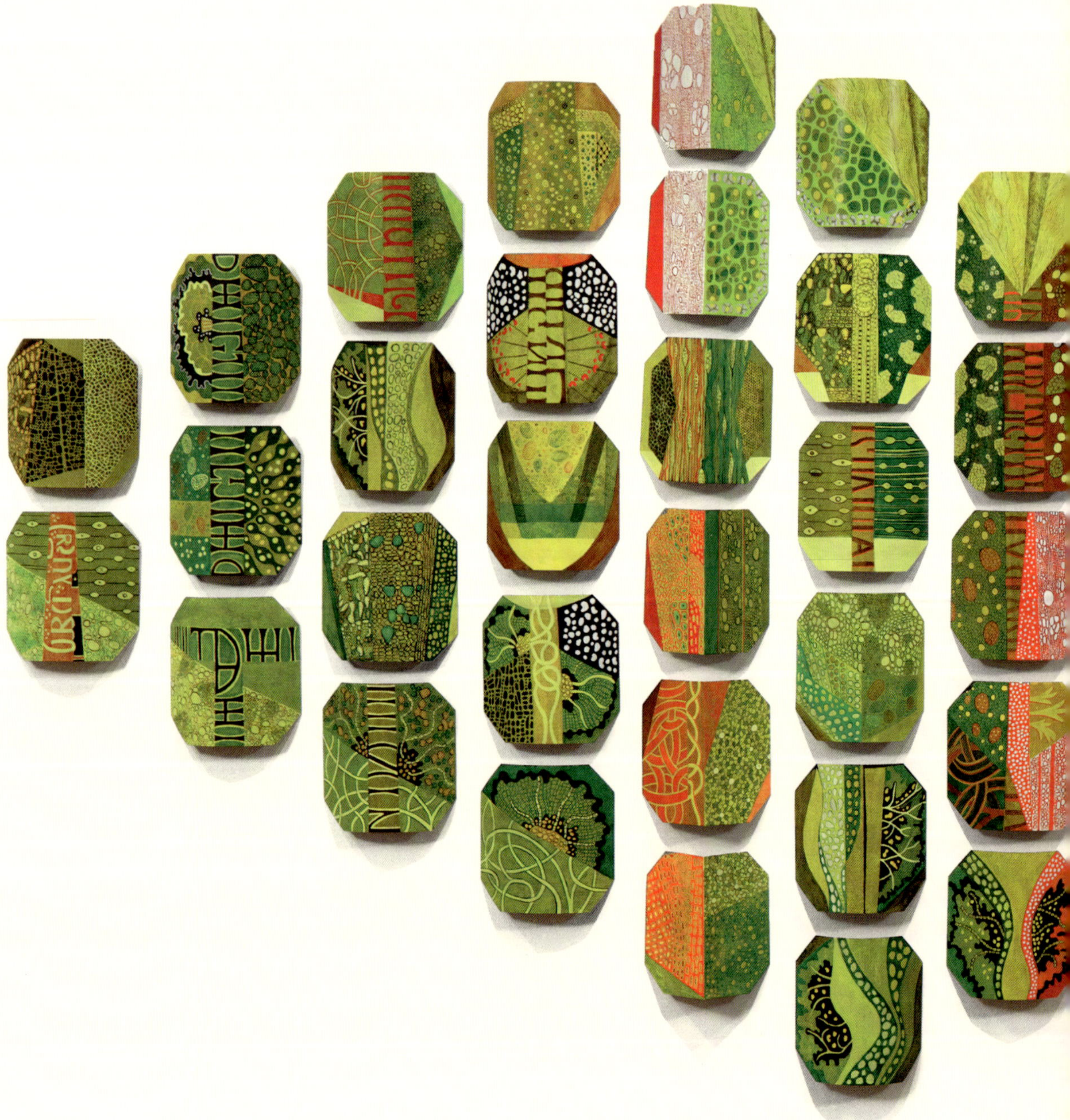

ESMÉ THOMPSON

THE ALCHEMY OF DESIGN

With contributions by
Liz Quackenbush and Marjorie Curry Woods
and an interview with the artist
by Brian Kennedy

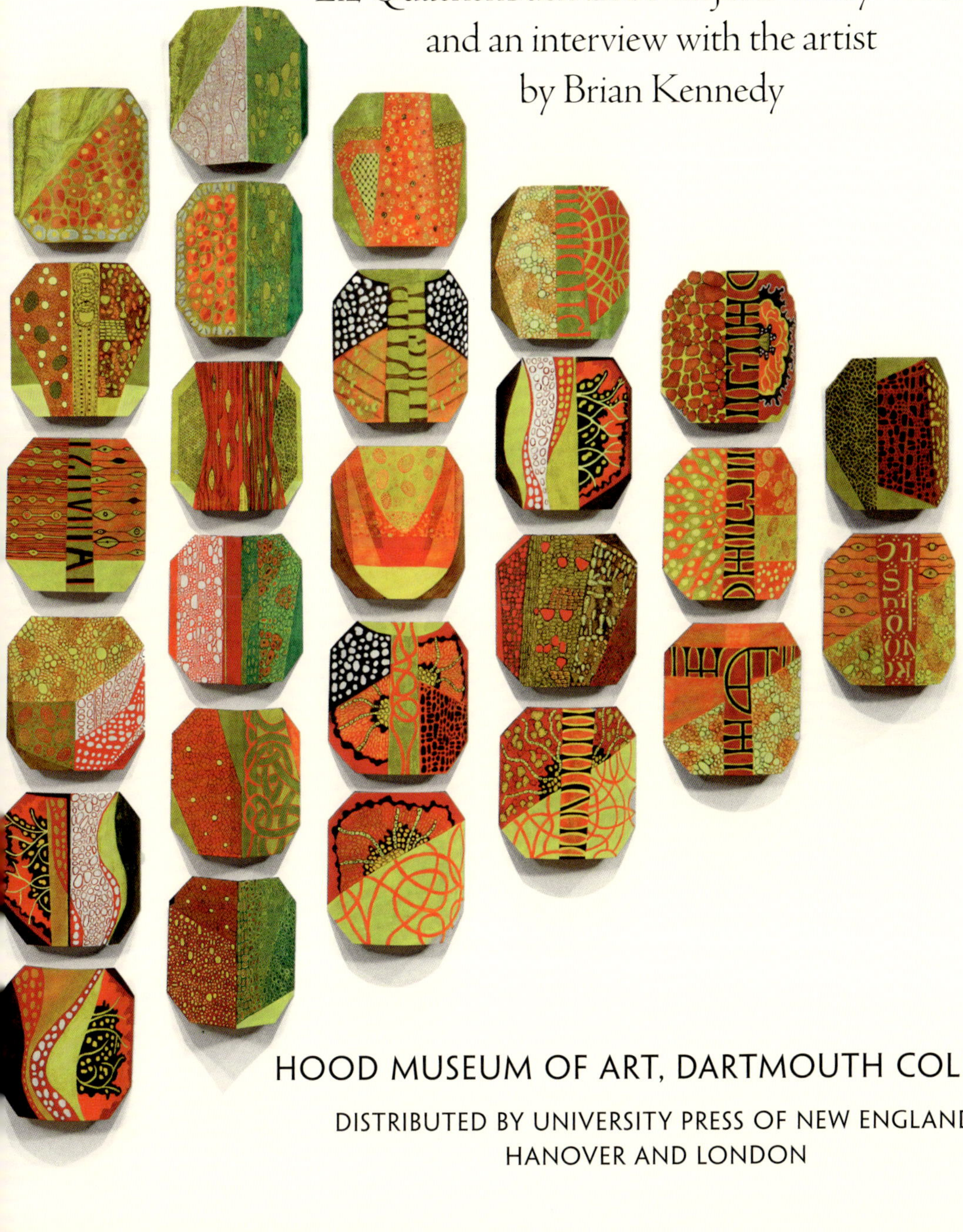

HOOD MUSEUM OF ART, DARTMOUTH COLLEGE

DISTRIBUTED BY UNIVERSITY PRESS OF NEW ENGLAND
HANOVER AND LONDON

Hood Museum of Art, Dartmouth College
Hanover, New Hampshire 03755
www.hoodmuseum.dartmouth.edu

Distributed by
University Press of New England
1 Court Street, Suite 250
Lebanon, New Hampshire 03766
www.upne.com

Esmé Thompson: The Alchemy of Design
Hood Museum of Art, Dartmouth College
Hanover, New Hampshire
April 9–May 29, 2011

This exhibition and catalogue were organized by the Hood Museum of Art and were generously supported by Kate and Yaz Krehbiel, Class of 1991, Thayer 1992, and the Bernard R. Siskind 1955 Fund.

Edited by Nils Nadeau
Designed by Margery Cantor
Printed by Capital Offset Company Inc.

All object photography is by Jeffrey Nintzel, unless otherwise indicated.
All works are in the collection of the artist, unless otherwise indicated.

Cover: Esmé Thompson, *Blue Divide* (detail), 2005, forty-nine-piece installation, acrylic on tin (concave galvanized maple sugar bucket lids), 94 x 194 x 3 inches. Hood Museum of Art, Dartmouth College: Purchased through the William S. Rubin Fund; 2008.11.

Back cover: *Blue Divide*, 2005.

Frontispiece: Esmé Thompson, *Djellaba* (detail), 2010, fifty-seven-piece installation, acrylic on metal, 94 x 194 x 3 inches. Collection of the artist.

Printed in the United States of America.

Library of Congress Cataloging-in-Publication Data

Thompson, Esmé (Pamela E.), 1946–
Esmé Thompson : The Alchemy of Design / With contributions by Liz Quackenbush and Marjorie Woods and an interview with the artist by Brian Kennedy.
p. cm
Issued in connection with an exhibition.
ISBN 978-0-944722-40-4
1. Thompson, Esmé, 1946—Exhibitions. I. Quackenbush, Liz. II. Woods, Marjorie (Marjorie Curry), 1947–III. Title.
N6537.T476A4 2011
709.2—dc22

Contents

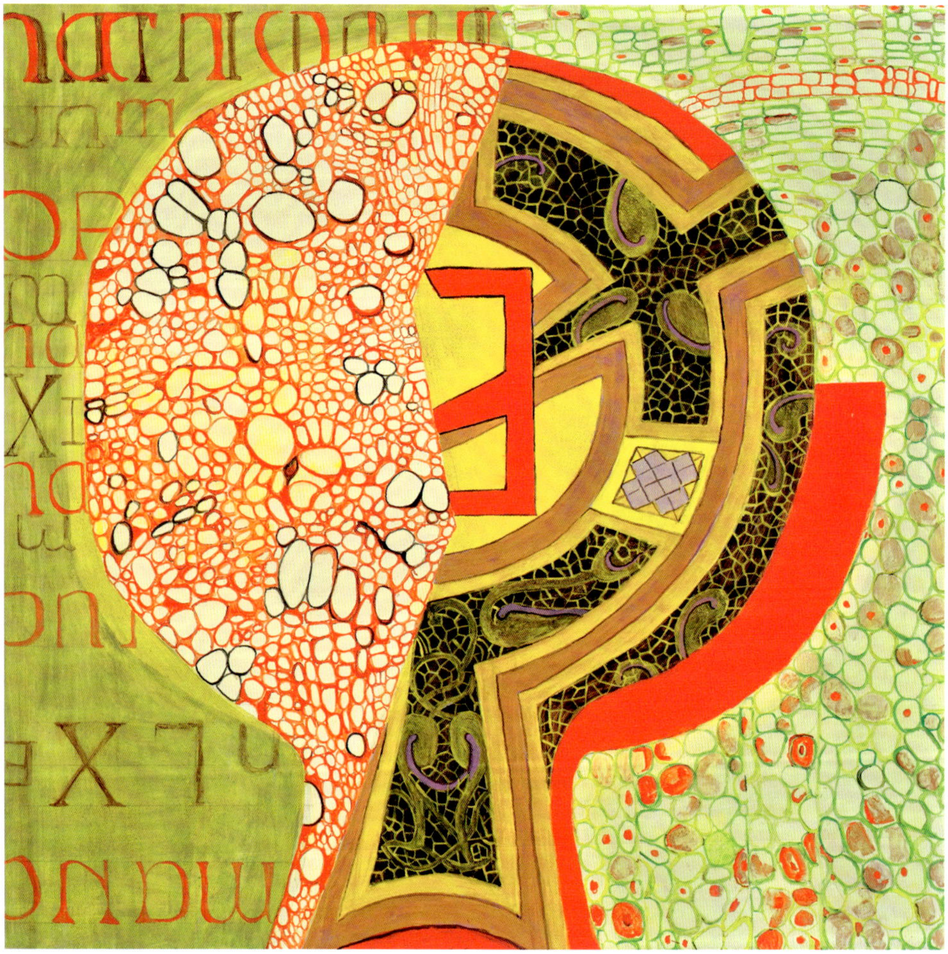

Credo, 2005, acrylic on board. Photography by Hathorne/Olson.

Preface and Acknowledgments

THIS book accompanies an exhibition of the art of Esmé Thompson, a creative and ebullient spirit in both her work and her life. The exhibition focuses on the last seven years of her creative practice and demonstrates the full flowering of her interest in design and pattern. It becomes apparent in the essays by medieval literature scholar Marjorie Curry Woods and ceramicist/artist Liz Quackenbush that Esmé Thompson envelops her creative enterprise in the colors and complexities to be found in the visual "surfaces" of textiles, illuminated manuscripts, and the botanical world. Her art also embraces the work of other painters whom she admires for these same interests, particularly Renaissance masters and the remarkably unique paintings of late-nineteenth- and early-twentieth-century French artist Edouard Vuillard.

This exhibition is, as well, a tribute to Esmé Thompson's career as a professor in Dartmouth College's Studio Art Department, where she has taught for the last three decades. Her colleagues at the museum and in the department celebrate the creativity of this distinguished artist through this showcasing of her recent paintings, collages, and ceramic work. I would first like to thank the artist, then, for her wonderful collaboration on this project; her frank and engaging personality, and the pleasure she has taken in working with the staff at the Hood, have been very evident, and we have truly appreciated her full participation in the creative enterprise of this exhibition. The members of the Hood staff who contributed to this effort include Patrick Dunfey, Exhibitions Designer, who visited the artist's studio and worked with her on the presentation; former Hood Director Brian Kennedy, for his engaging interview with the artist; Nils Nadeau, Communications and Publications Manager, who edited and oversaw this book; Kathleen O'Malley, Acting Collections Manager and Associate Registrar, who arranged for the transportation and photography of the art; and last but far from least, Essi Rönkkö, Assistant Curator for Special Projects, who worked at one time or another on every aspect of the book and exhibition, including compiling the checklist itself. Freelance photographer Jeffrey Nintzel shot almost all of the work in the book, graphic designer Margery Cantor contributed the book's beautiful design, and Kristin Rose transcribed the interview. We thank Liz Quackenbush and Marjorie Curry Woods for their insightful essays in tribute to the work of their colleague Esmé Thompson, and Brenda Garand for her support of the artist and members of the Studio Art Department faculty. The artist would also like to thank the Liguria Study Center for the Arts and Humanities, the John Sloan Dickey Center for International Understanding, and the Leslie Center for the Humanities for providing research and travel grants, and Professor Quackenbush and Doug Peltzman for their support for the ceramic work. Lastly, this exhibition would not have been possible without the great generosity of Kate and Yaz Krehbiel, Class of 1991, Thayer 1992, who are very supportive of the museum and the long legacy of teachers in the arts at Dartmouth College.

Katherine Hart
Interim Director
Barbara C. and Harvey P. Hood 1918
Curator of Academic Programming

ESMÉ THOMPSON

THE ALCHEMY OF DESIGN

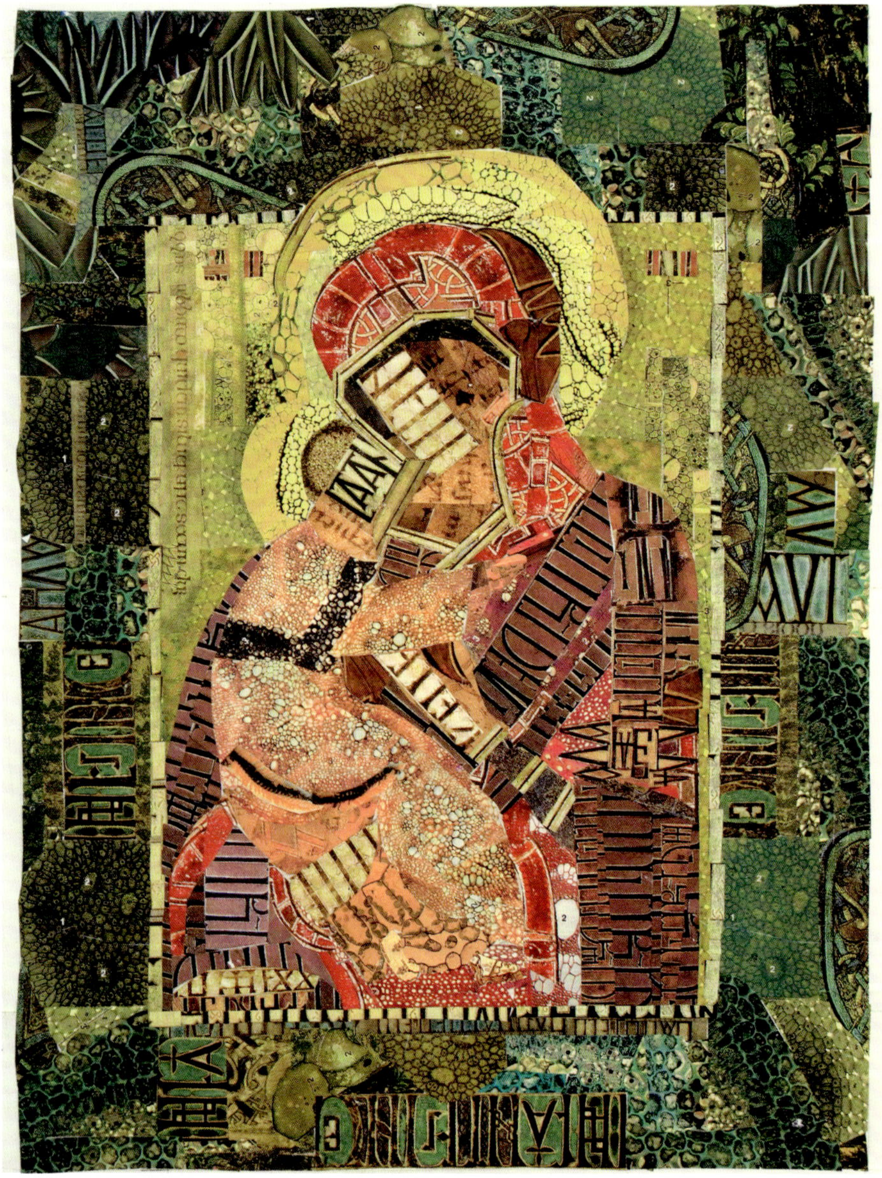

Above: *Madonna and Child,* 2007, collage.

Opposite: 1.1. Robert Campin (ca. 1375/9–1444), *The Annunciation Triptych (Merode Altarpiece),* ca. 1425, oil on wood. The Metropolitan Museum of Art, The Cloisters Collection, 1956 (56.70). Image copyright © The Metropolitan Museum of Art / Art Resource, NY

1

Mediating the Medieval (and More)

MARJORIE CURRY WOODS

ESMÉ Thompson's work is complex and always evolving, the product of a life of expanding experiences and influences. Diverse strands appear in individual works, while specific threads persist throughout her oeuvre. Most familiar to me are the medieval and Renaissance influences, ranging from the wings of Annunciation angels to Sienese painted wooden book covers and folios of illuminated manuscripts almost too beautiful to read. These appear over and over in her works. The originators of such medieval objects—painters and illustrators as well as scribes and writers—were trained through long apprenticeship or formal education spent imitating and echoing the works of previous masters. Appreciative (but also ruthless) use of the work of artists who have come before is typical of premodern creativity, but it is also a hallmark of modern masters.[1] Like them, Thompson dips constantly into the historical well, returning again and again to her favorite sources.

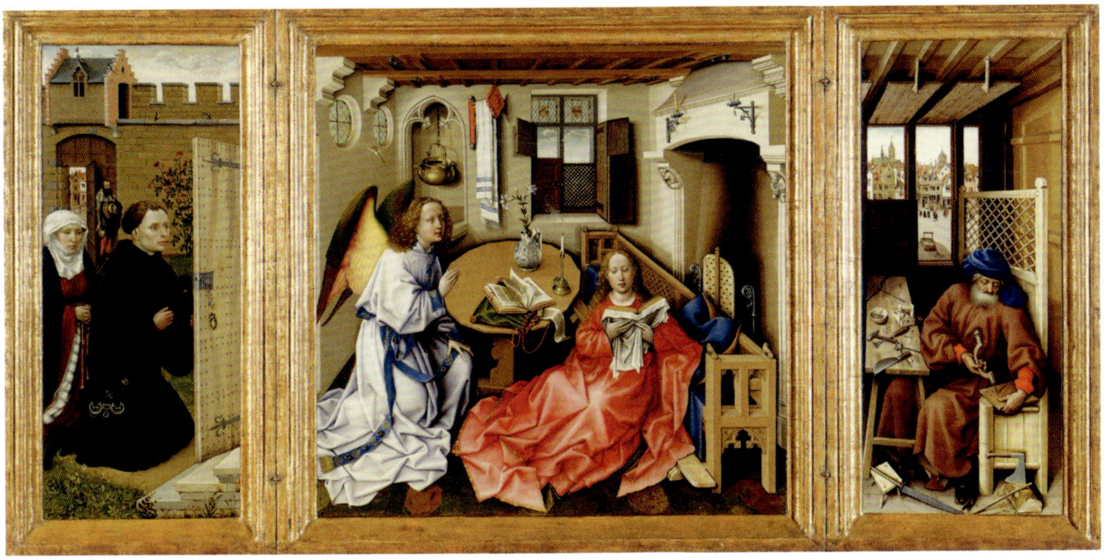

Both the content and the structure of depictions of the Annunciation have fascinated Thompson throughout her career. The famous *Annunciation* triptych (1427–32) in the Cloisters from the workshop of Robert Campin, the Master of Flémalle, has been a consistent source of inspiration (fig. 1.1). One of the most memorable elements of the genre of Annunciation painting is the body profile of the winged angel on the left; he is coming to tell the Virgin Mary, who is reading on the right, that she will be the mother of the son of God. The gorgeous asymmetrical shape of an angel's wing appears without narrative context in a number of Thompson's large paintings from the mid-1990s. In examples such as *Locus IV* or *Flap II* (1996), a single wing appears on the left of the composition, while in slightly later works like *Web* (1997; fig. 1.2) or *Memento Mori II* (1998), the shape occurs in a mirrored symmetrical structure with varied size and pattern. Thompson returned

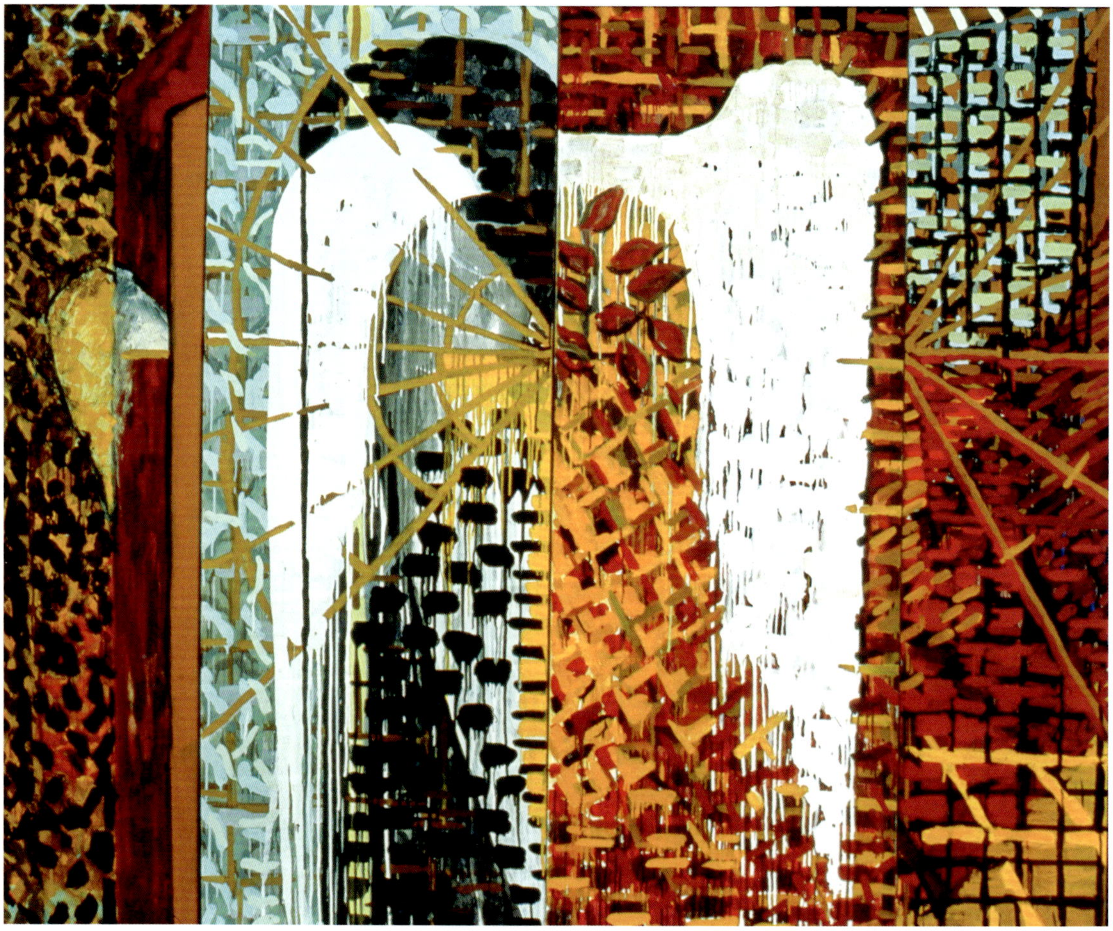

1.2. *Web*, 1997, oil on four canvases. Photography by Slide Specialists.

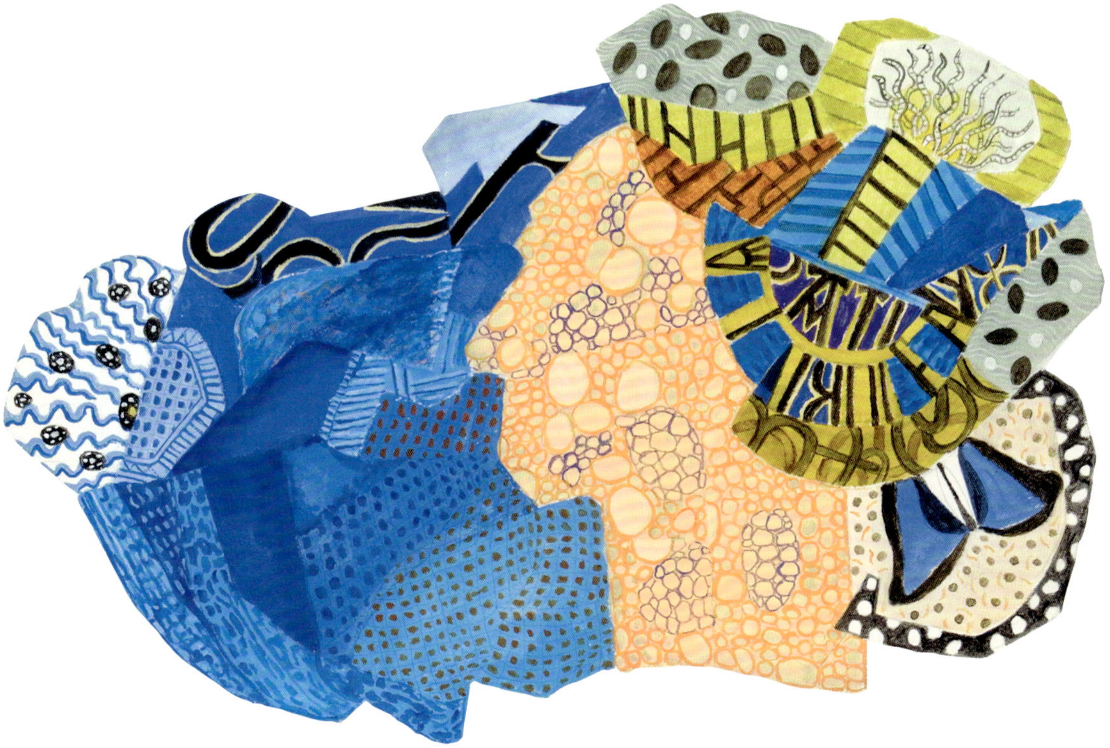

1.3. *Bogliasco Shadow*, 2008, acrylic on paper. Photography by Hathorne/Olson.

to Campin's *Annunciation* over and over, not only for its formal elements but also for her developing interest in adjoining panels and pieces with multiple interacting parts. Thompson found particularly inspiring its final triptych form, which encompasses side panels now thought to have been executed in stages.[2] Several of her significant installations in other locations, such as *Cycles* (1984) in the Lamont Gallery of the Frederick Mayer Art Center at Phillips Exeter Academy, reflect the monumentality and rich, deep beauty—and even some of the color palette—of the Campin work (see fig. 2.2).

Much more recently, the majestic *Djellaba* installation (2010) is an important example of Thompson's current use of panel painting that reflects a mixture of inspirations (see fig. 2.9). Here she integrates medieval influences with more recent experiences in Morocco with *zellij* tiles and North African carpet weaving. The term *djellaba* refers to the long robes woven by Berber women but worn by members of both sexes. Thompson says of this installation,

> I like the idea of weaving color, form, and pattern in my work much as do the textiles and mosaics I love so much. The outside shape of the piece itself reminds me of the

shape of not only the *djellaba* robes but also the robes that Matisse designed for the Chapelle du Rosaire de Vence. This is a new palette for me, a vibrant, complementary palette of red to green mirroring.[3]

The shifting pattern of color counterpoints the overlapping and interconnecting formal elements, resulting in an organic whole that reflects the diversity as well a powerful integration of the originary elements.

During the last decade, the small, quiet Italian town of Bogliasco has become a recurring refuge and special source of inspiration for Thompson. In this seaside suburb east of the sprawl and action of Genoa is located the Centro Studi Ligure, a tiny residence for writers and artists in a villa on the edge of the Mediterranean. She has visited and revisited Bogliasco, whose waters and depths are reflected, along with her interest in Italian female portraiture, in *Bogliasco Shadow* (2008; fig. 1.3). I met Esmé Thompson at Bogliasco in 1999. During a research trip to Siena at that time to examine rhetoric manuscripts, I first encountered *biccherne*: thick and elaborately painted and decorated wooden book covers that had been used to protect documents in the city treasury during the later Middle Ages (fig. 1.4).[4] Originally belonging to the Palazzo Pubblico of Siena but gradually dispersed, many of these historically and culturally significant artifacts have been gathered back together and are now exhibited in an upper-floor gallery of the Archivio di Stato. These small panels resemble, not only in their dimensions but also often in their patterns of interior division and decoration, the sequences of paintings that Thompson had been doing—after much experimentation—on the metal tops of maple sugar buckets (fig. 1.5). I urged her to go to Siena, where the *biccherne* captivated her, too. They have been a major source of inspiration for her ever since, and she has become something of an expert on this distinctive and unique medieval genre.

Each of Thompson's painted metal pieces can be appreciated on its own, but her group installations of these pieces create an almost hypnotic variation of patterns and colors, as in *Ornamentum V* (2005; plate 4), where the vertical lines of the deceptively simple yet rich spectrum transcend the divisions among the pieces. In larger installations such as *Blue Divide* (also 2005; see plate 5 and the cover of this book), the more complicated interrelationships and interconnecting patterns demand even more attention. While the complex structure of *Blue Divide* is purely formal, the slightly earlier *Beatus II* (2003; fig. 1.6 and plate 1), meaning "blessed," has a symbolic cruciform structure that evokes a central aspect of medieval Christianity. *Beatus* is the installation most specifically related to the secular *biccherne*, but the other inspiration for it was an illustration in a medieval Book of Hours depicting the division of the world into three strata signifying heaven, earth, and hell—a simple color pattern that led Thompson to her installation's internal formal organization.

For some of her multi-piece metal installations, Thompson makes the link to verbal rhetoric obvious in titles such as *Metonymy* (1999), *Synecdoche* (1999), *Chiasmus* (2002), and *Epiploce* (2006). Metonymy is one of the most important of the tropes (which use language in a non-literal way) and draws on the associative power of the creative intellect. In simplest terms, it is a "reference to something or someone by naming one of its attributes."[5] With any trope, what is meant is more than what is literally stated, and we are thus invited to look at its context in a new way. In Thompson's installation *Metonymy*, various references and allusions pull us back and forth throughout the work, encouraging us to make cognitive jumps while still in the artist's thrall.

In contrast to tropes, figures of diction identify a specific pattern in the words. Chiasmus, for example, is an expression in which ideas or grammatical structures are repeated in inverted order: the end takes us back to the beginning and follows a tight path within a narrow compass. In Thompson's work of this title (fig. 1.7), forty-eight metal panels are joined in the center by an implied yellow "V." The panels are arranged in a mirrored design with a warm orange side on the left and a cool grey/blue side on the right; most of the

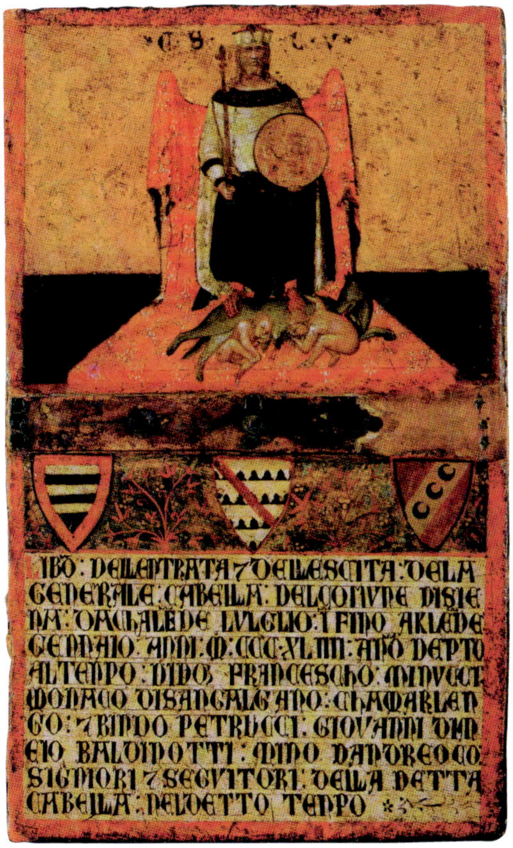

1.4. Ambrogio Lorenzetti (ca. 1290–1348), *Good Government*, 1344, oil on wood. Biccherna no 16, Museo delle biccherne, Archivio di Stato, Siena.

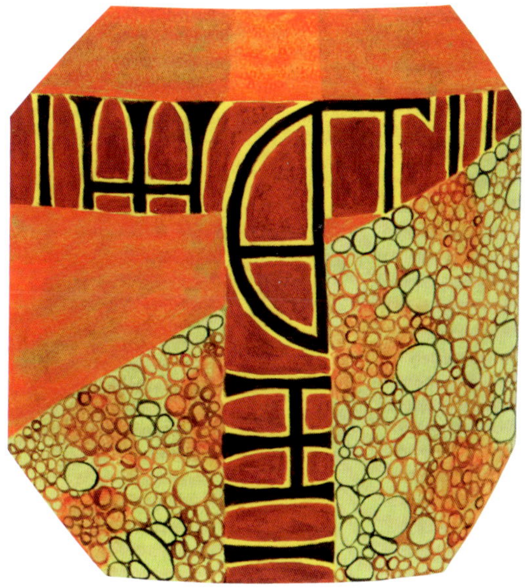

1.5. *Above: Djellaba* (detail), 2010, fifty-seven-piece installation, acrylic on metal, panel 12 x 12 x 3 inches.

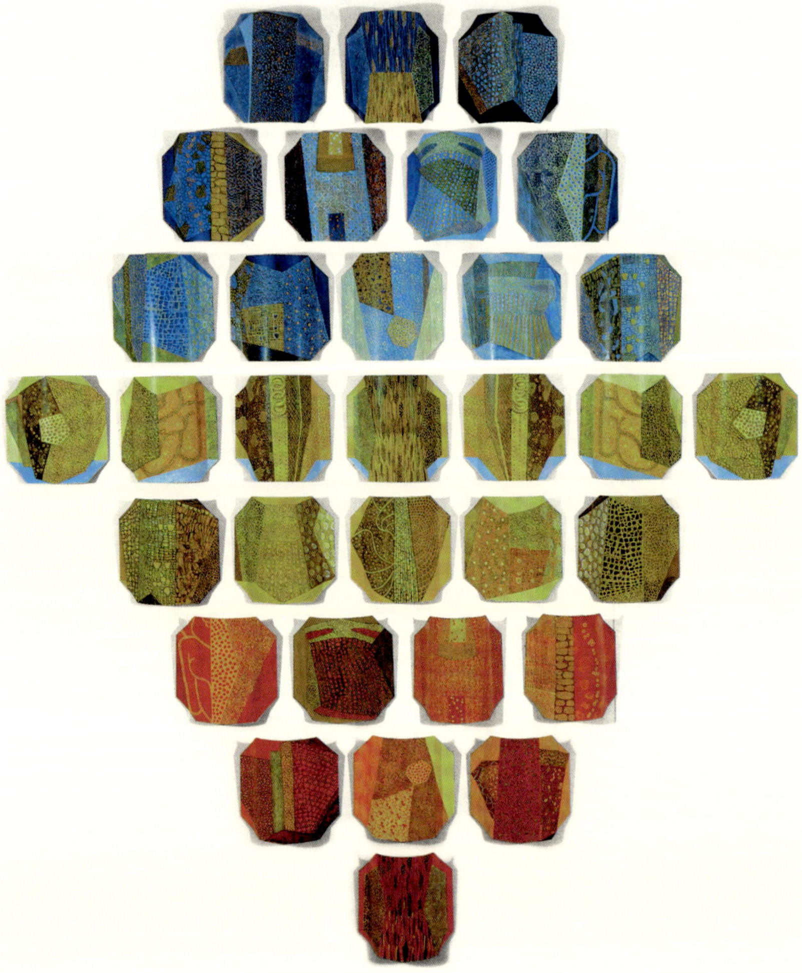

1.6. *Beatus*, 2003, thirty-two-piece installation; acrylic on metal, 69 x 42 x 3 inches.

images directly opposite each other are mirror reversals in both color and design. The internal dynamic of the work engages the viewer in discerning the multiple visual pairs.

In these titles she uses terms that come from the premodern analysis of verbal texts, but words themselves do not appear. More recently, however, she has incorporated fragments of verbal texts inspired by medieval manuscripts and Byzantine icons. Medieval scribes and painters emphasized the aesthetic as well as the intellectual impact of the written word. When I was first working on manuscripts, I was told that the English word "text" comes from the Latin *textus*, meaning "woven," because of the desire of medieval scribes to make written words on the page look like a pattern, and German Gothic script is often referred to as *textura* because of its interwoven look (the bane of palaeography students ever since). Similarly, the word *pagina* can mean "rows of vines joined together," where "the lines on the page were the thread of a trellis which supports the vines."[6] It is these curvilinear, constructed, woven qualities of letter and image that Thompson responds to, as well as the resonance of the color and the way that an image can be buried in or combined with lettering. She crops or fragments the textual allusions in her works in order to focus on the design of the words rather than their meaning.

The splendid, mammoth ninth-century Book of Kells has had a major influence on Thompson's most current work. The complexity of execution and use of verbal units as

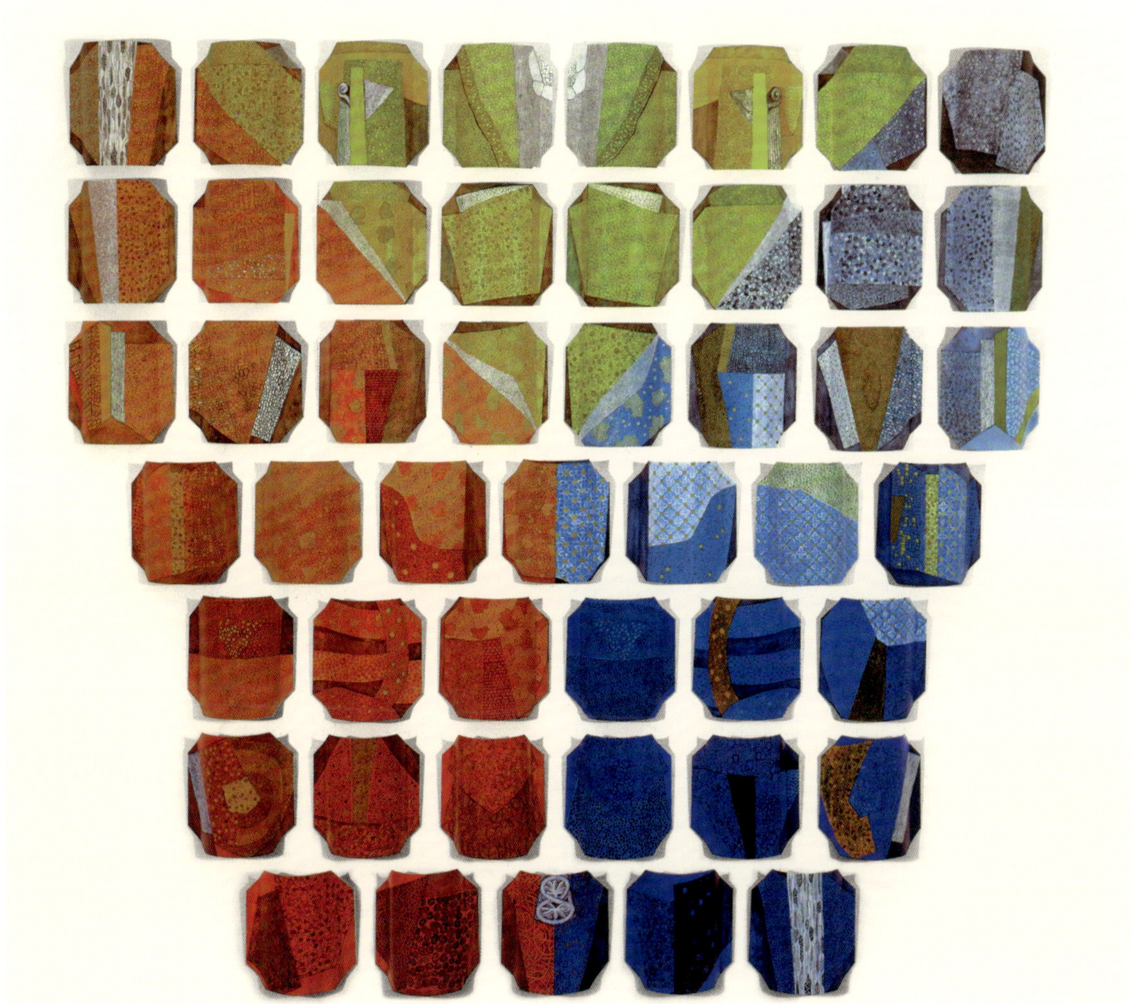

1.7. *Chiasmus*, 2002, forty-eight-piece installation, acrylic on metal, 102 x 117 x 3 inches. Photography by Andrew Daubenspeck.

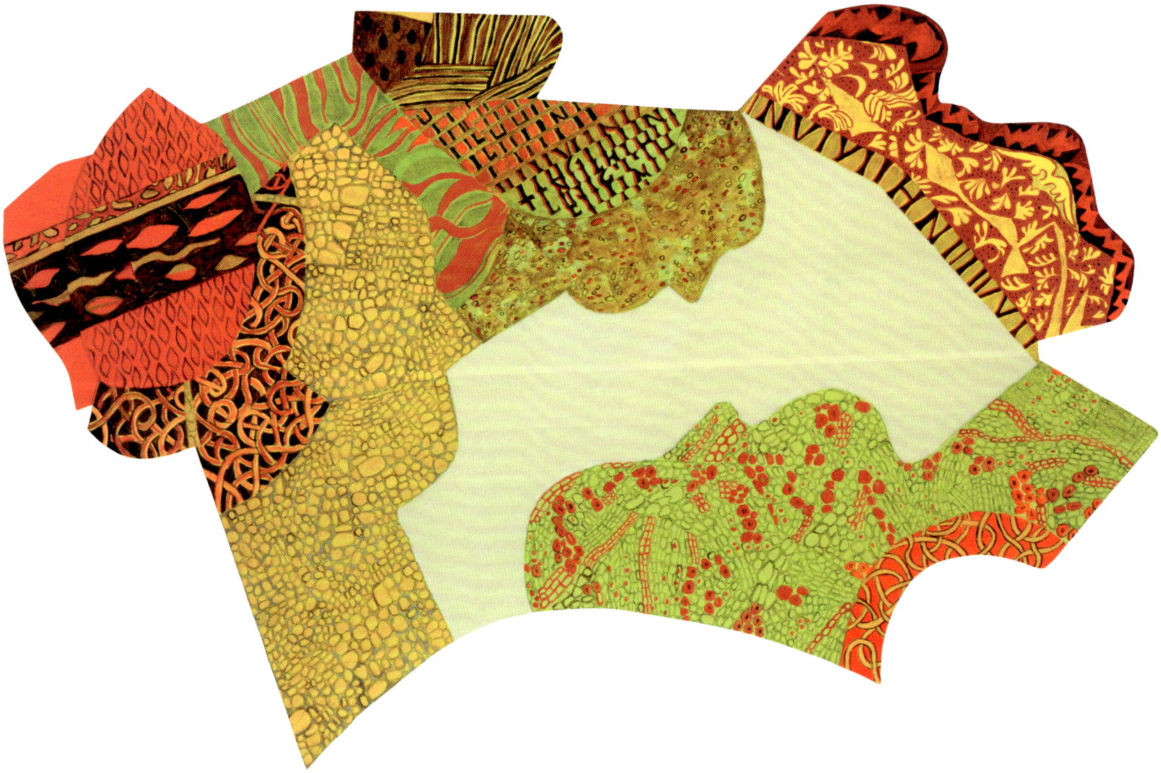

1.8. *Trio V*, 2010, acrylic and oil on board.

visual content in this famous manuscript are reflected in a number of Thompson's painting and collage works of the new century, and the layered text and interwoven scrollwork represent a particular inspiration. Her very new piece, *Trio V* (2010; fig. 1.8), is a shaped painting on board in which the figures move inward from the outside edge. Many of its text and knot patterns, as well as the intricate patterns of red, gold, and black and the organic forms, are drawn from one of the folios of the Gospel of Luke in the Book of Kells.[7]

When Thompson finds a pattern she likes, she reuses it for years. It may begin in a collage and then be reinterpreted in a painting and then be transformed or recycled in further pieces as well. Thompson becomes interested in the work of an earlier artist for its structure or use of space when she feels that there is something that she can learn from it. The resonance that a particular source has for her remains somewhat mysterious while continuing to inform and enliven her work. She usually starts by creating a collage or small painting based on it. After that, however, she builds on her own responses, and

1.9. Opposite: *Liggia I*, 2003, acrylic on canvas.

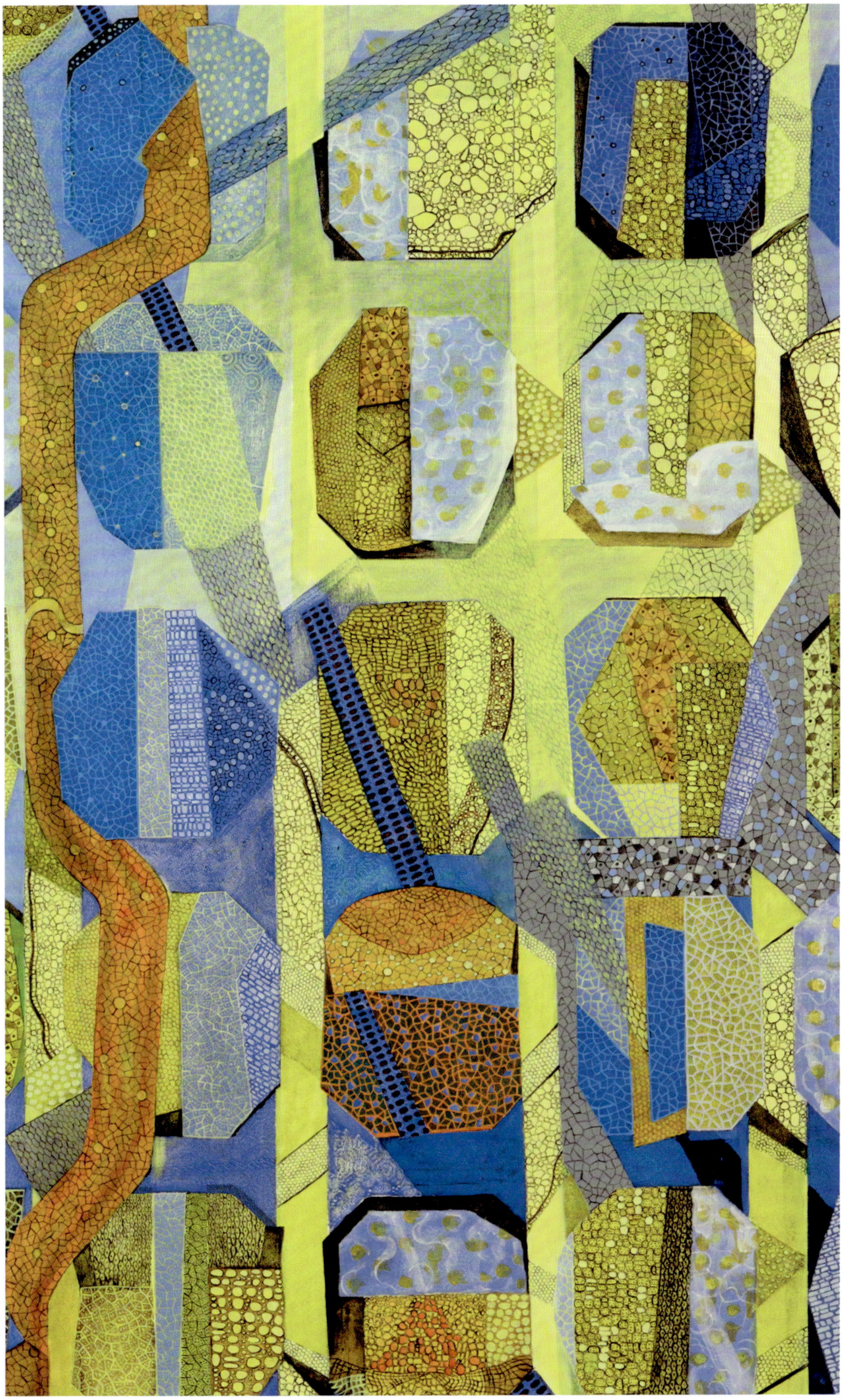

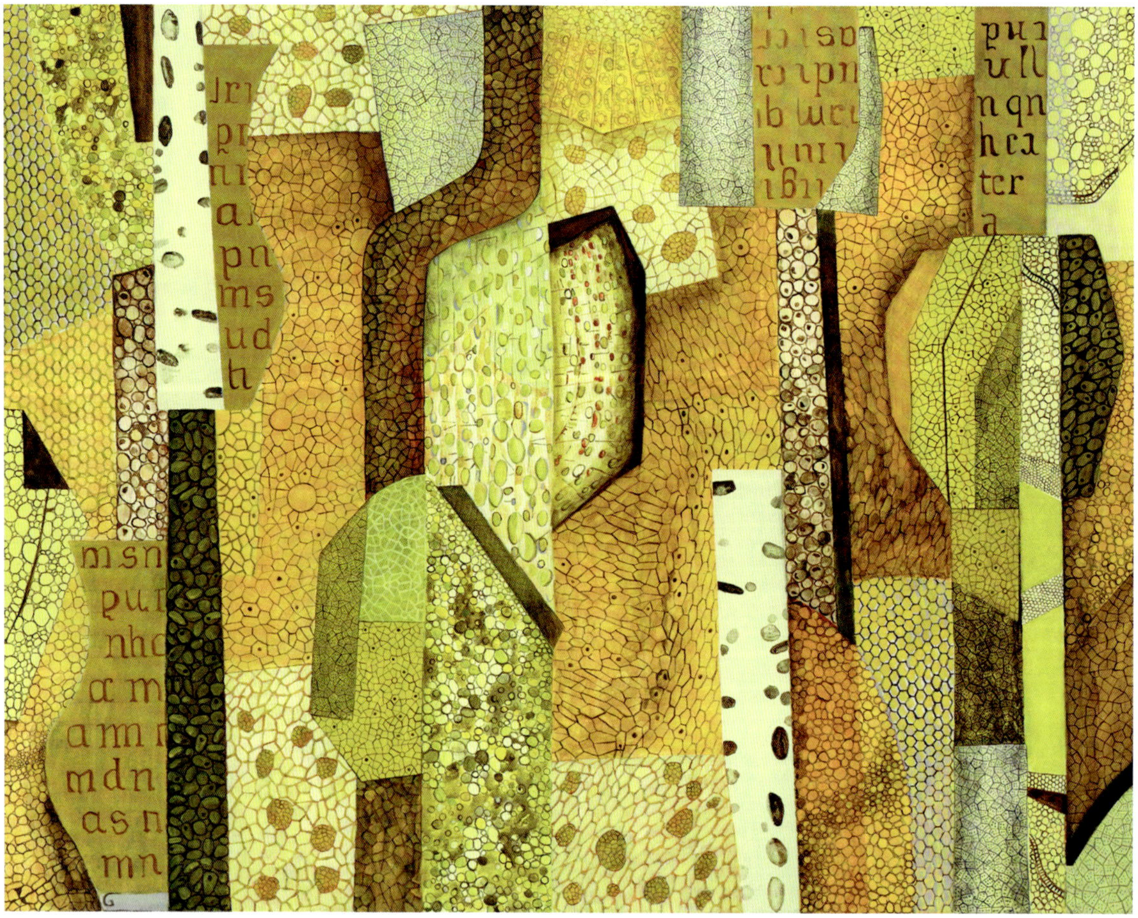

1.10. *Tessere I*, 2004, acrylic on canvas.

the final result has evolved and been transformed in color and structure. For example, she has worked with Edouard Vuillard's *The Flowered Dress* since 2005. Almost all of the *Annaghmakerrig* (see fig. 2.6) paintings and collages are derived from it, and she has also elaborated on it in a new ceramic piece, *Portal* (2010). Yet through the evolution of space and color, only a few of the original references remain. Picasso said of his response to the works of other artists, "When I begin a picture, there is somebody who works with me. Toward the end, I get the impression that I have been working alone—without a collaborator"; this results in what Susan Galassi calls a "dialogic form" of creativity.[8]

Sometimes Thompson's dialogues are with her earlier self. In keeping with her revision and rethinking of her earlier works, the collective shapes of the individual pieces

1.11. Opposite: *Cleopatra*, 2008, acrylic on board. Photography by Hathorne/Olson.

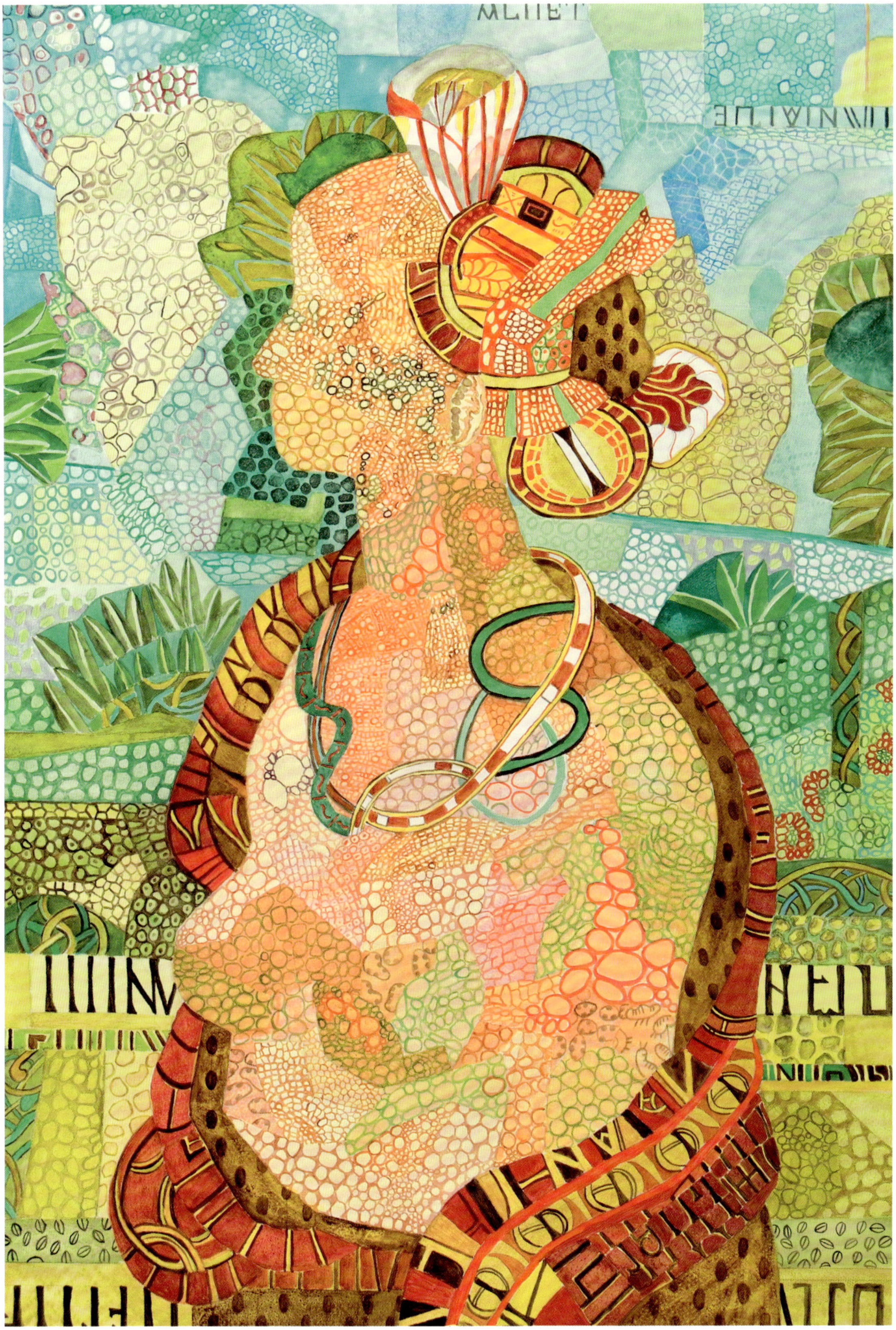

in her metal installations appear in painterly form in *Liggia I* (2003; fig. 1.9), where the former interstices between individual objects in the metal installations become part of the picture, a technique further evolved in *Liggia III* (2004). Likewise, she reworks the shapes and designs of her metal installations in combination with verbal elements in the compositional mix of *Tessere I* (2004; fig. 1.10). The narrow bands of pattern here emphasize the truncation of the words and highlight the medieval letter forms, which were often much more individualized and elegant than those produced later by the printing press. The textually oriented observer will be attracted by these elements but frustrated in any attempt to "read" the words, which must instead be seen as but one part of a much more complex visual construct. In *Annaghmakerrig V* (2005, see fig. 2.6), the variety of scripts combined with the vertical as well as horizontal positioning of lettered elements let us know immediately that the words are formal constructs.

Smaller bits and pieces of text are "buried" in Thompson's recent collages, which draw formal elements from Renaissance portraits of aristocratic women. Among the paintings and collages devoted to female figures, both secular and divine, are *Madonna and*

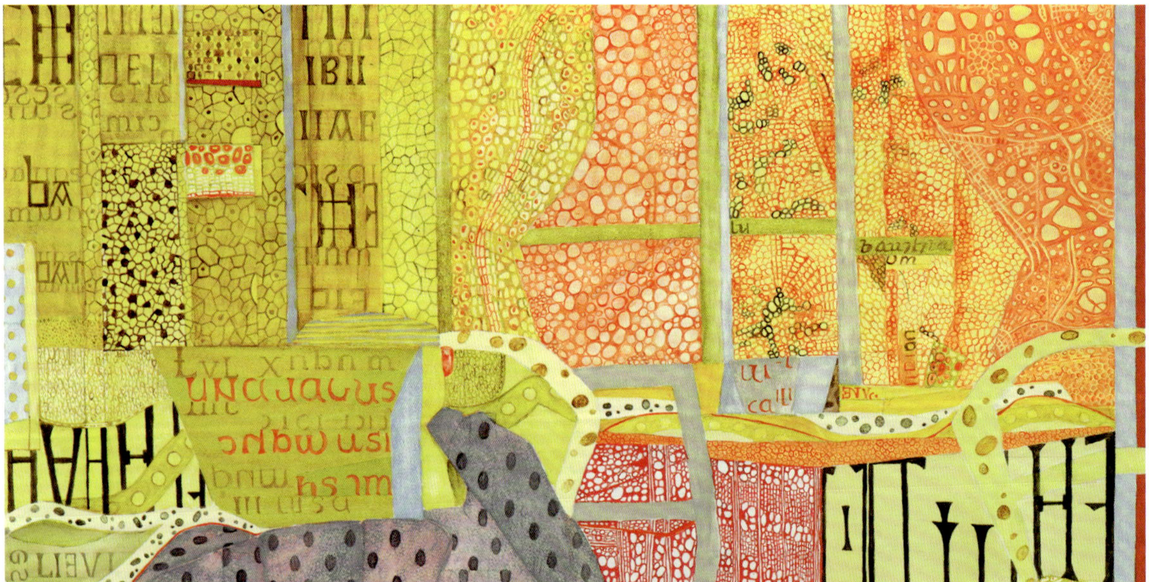

1.12. *Lisant III*, 2006, acrylic on board.

Child (2007; see the beginning of this essay), which evokes Byzantine icons, *Incontriamo*, and *Donna* (2008; plates 10 and 11). Pisanello's portrait of Ginevra D'Este was the inspiration for *After Pisanello* (2007; plate 6), and Piero di Cosimo's *Portrait of Simonetta Vespucchi* for *Cleopatra* (2008; fig. 1.11). Edouard Vuillard's *Madame Vuillard Reading the Newspaper* (1898) inspired the *Lisant* ("reading") series (fig. 1.12).

Esmé Thompson shares with medieval artists and writers a creative response to inspirations both new and old. Medieval artists of Western Europe were quick to adopt novel trends and influences, such as those emanating from the Byzantine and Muslim worlds, even as they worked over and over with traditional Celtic and Roman sources. Likewise, medieval students learning Latin in schools rewrote both the works of antiquity and what were to them the new, contemporary classics of Latin poetry. A common assignment was to rework part of a well-known story, such as the beginning of one of Ovid's interwoven narratives in the *Metamorphoses*. Indeed, the concept of metamorphosis itself—the mutation of shapes into a prolix variety of forms—was particularly fascinating to the medieval imagination. That sense of creativity is revived in the works of Thompson, whose craftsmanship has been honed by contact with a succession of rich sources of inspiration that she breaks apart and recreates in her own visual vocabulary. The formal sophistication and beauty of her work make an immediate impression that is only deepened by the recognition of the rich multiplicity of cultural influences at play there.

NOTES

1. See, for example, Susan Grace Galassi, *Picasso's Variations on the Masters: Confrontations with the Past* (New York: Harry N. Abrams, 1996).
2. See http://www.metmuseum.org/toah/works-of-art/56.70 (accessed October 7, 2010).
3. Email correspondence with the author, August 7, 2010.
4. See *Le Biccherne di Siena: arte e finanza all/alba dell'economia moderna*, ed. Alessandro Tomei (Rome: Retablo, 2002). On Siena, Archivio di Stato, 41, see p. 218, with a plate on 219. There is an excellent detailed description of a single *biccherna* at the Victoria and Albert Museum that also includes an informative history of the genre in English, available at http://collections.vam.ac.uk/item/O132680/tempera-painting-tavoletta-di-biccherna-the-camarlingo/?print=1# (accessed October 7, 2010).
5. See *Silva Rhetoricae: The Forest of Rhetoric*, s.v."metonymy" and "chiasmus," available at http://rhetoric.byu.edu/ (accessed October 7, 2010).
6. Ivan Illich, *In the Vineyard of the Text: A Commentary to Hugh's Didascalicon* (Chicago: University of Chicago Press, 1993), 57.
7. Other notable manuscript influences on Thompson's work include the Incarnation initial from the Lindisfarne Gospels and the "Carpet Page" from the Book of Durrow.
8. Galassi, *Picasso's Variations*, 19.

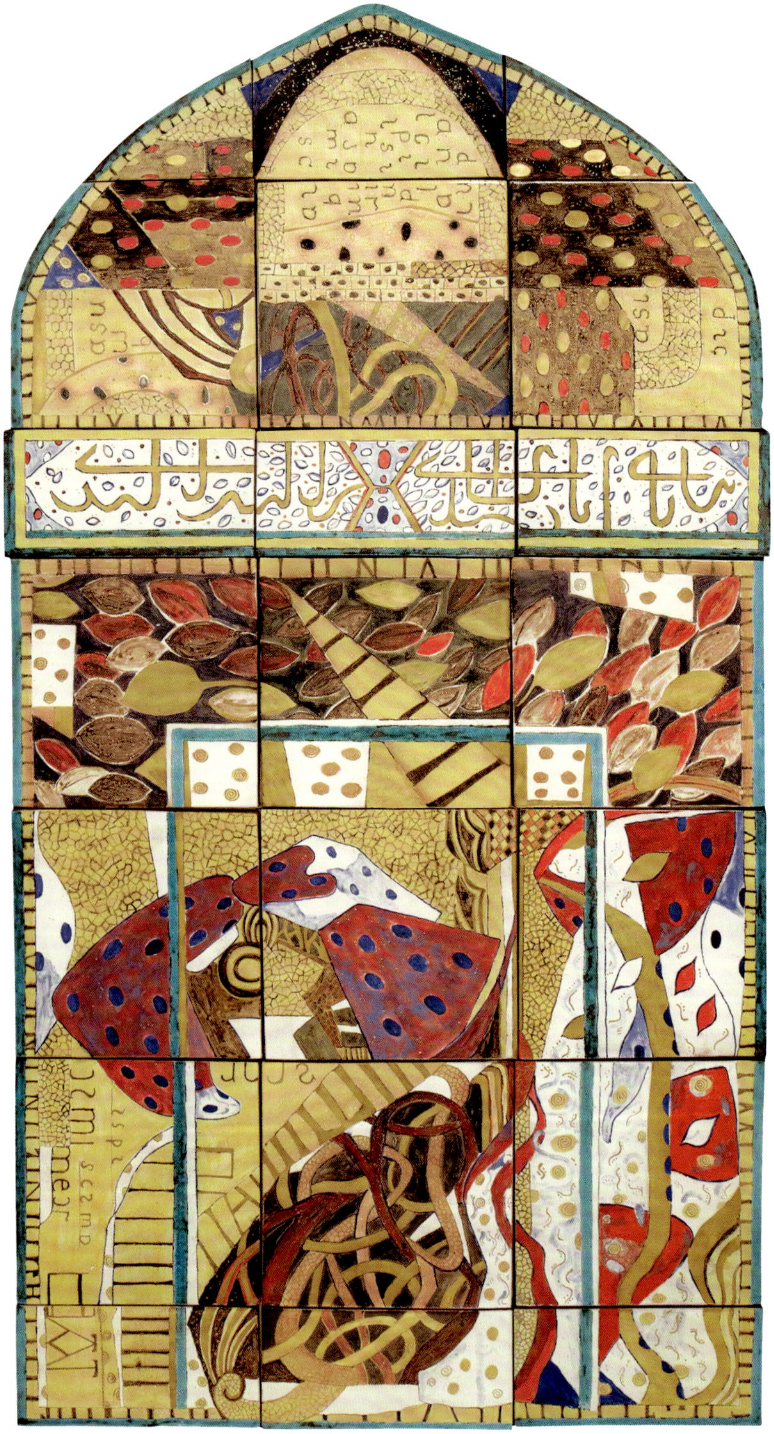

Portal, 2010, twenty-one ceramic *maiolica* tiles.

2.1. Opposite: Esmé's garden. Photography by Esmé Thompson.

2

Reflections

LIZ QUACKENBUSH

> You see, I believe that one ought always to regard a garden in terms of architecture as well as of colour. One has huge lumps of, let us say, the shrub roses making large voluminous bushes like a Victorian crinoline, or flinging themselves in wild sprays; or putting it another way, some plants make round fat bushes, and seem to demand a contrast in a tall sharp plant, say delphiniums, sticking up in a cathedral sprays of bright blue amongst the roses instead of in the orthodox way at the back of a herbaceous border. It is all a question of shape.
>
> —Vita Sackville-West, in *Private Gardens*[1]

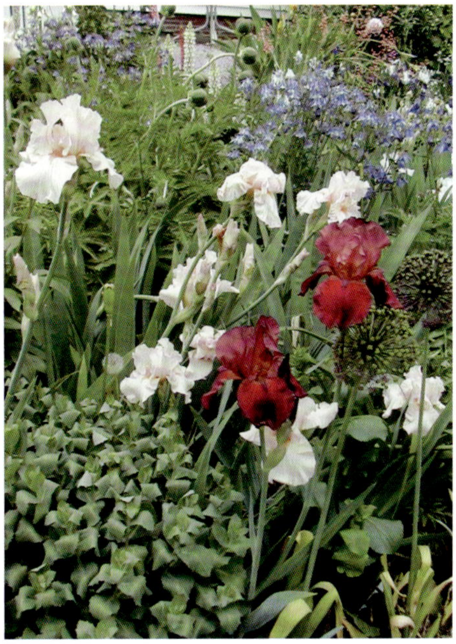

THE first time I entered one of Esmé Thompson's gardens, I was deeply moved by the mystical enchantment of the lush, soil-carpeted habitat, filled to the brim as it was with cohabitating vegetable and floral varieties. I recall tender lettuces growing in the shade of enormous yellow spiral-centered sunflowers, and bulbous two-toned lavender poppies pushing their way through the thorned branches of tea roses. Tall purplish-blue cone-shaped delphinium blossoms stood beside orange and hot pink zinnias. Globe thistles punctuated the spaces surrounding evening primrose. Purple irises leaned on staked yellow dahlias, which had just wintered over (as do many good ideas). Now they came out of hibernation. All of the plants seemed to breathe and sweat. No

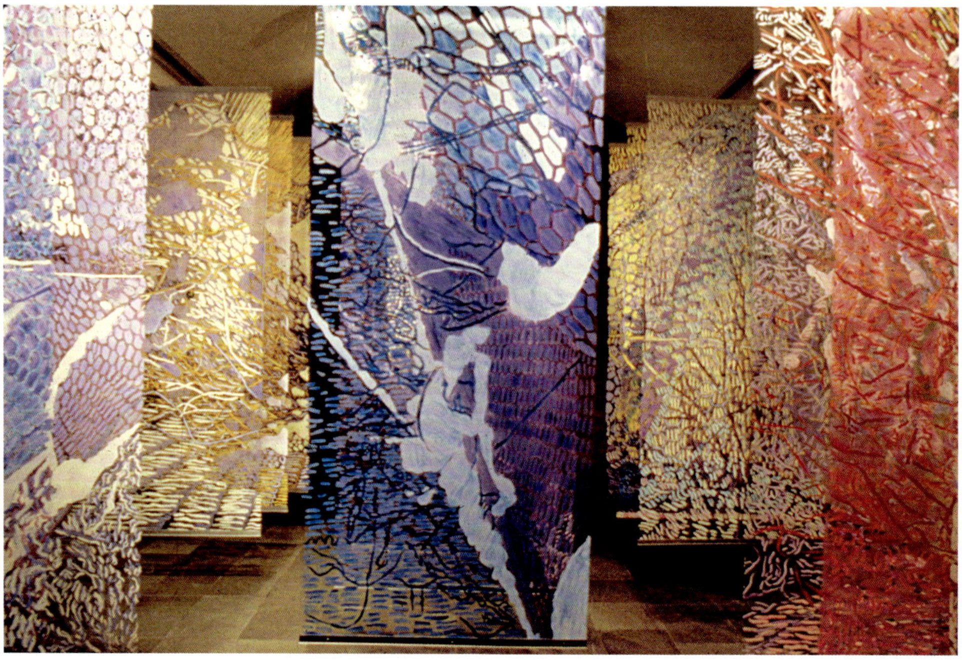

2.2. *Cycles*, 1984, installation at Lamont Gallery, Frederick Mayer Art Center, Phillips Exeter Academy, Exeter, N.H. Photography by Esmé Thompson.

weeds, no yellow leaves, only deep brown soil hosting a gathering that was bursting with life. The garden made Esmé's whimsy tangible, as its many colors and textures commingled and enhanced one another (fig. 2.1).

Esmé lives in her garden as she does in her studio, moving through its uniquely organized spaces, entirely at home with its manifestations of form, shape, color, and design. In fact, her painting process and iconography aligns itself with her gardening process; she immerses herself in complexity, and out of this abundance of opportunity derives design. I remember Esmé working on an installation of over one hundred four-by-eight-foot hanging acrylic screens, as she created a landscape painting of her garden that one could actually move through. The *Cycles* installation was shown in four galleries at Phillips Exeter Academy's Lamont Gallery in Exeter, New Hampshire, in 1984 (fig. 2.2); each room depicted a different season in the garden. Each room's dozens of clear plastic hanging panels did away with both the artistic ground (normally canvas) and the real ground, presenting only a shifting labyrinth of bold brush strokes that evoked the textures and colors of a space of blooming and beauty. Critic Robert Taylor writes:

> Esmé Thompson's is partly a durational experience, like listening to music or reading a narrative. Only when you've entered the installation is it possible to perceive the

> work's structural coherence . . . The spirit of *Cycles* is decorative, but decoration that has infinitely more to it than surface embellishment.[2]

After all, Esmé's art has always asked: "How can a painting move you through space, rather than refer to space, and how can the decorative arts function as the structure that creates this movement?"

Like the patterns in her garden, those of the domestic realm, the home of many of the decorative arts, also fascinate Esmé. She often turns to women's decorative traditions despite the longtime artworld prejudice against them, which is based on the false hierarchies of fine art above decorative art, Western art above non-Western art, men's art above women's art.[3] Esmé actively undermines such hierarchies in her painting. Using patterns from lace, embroidery, and weaving, she celebrates the traditional decorative arts of the home and those practitioners of them who embrace beauty for beauty's sake alone. She adapts certain traditional patterns and invents others, then allows them all to morph, collapse, and collide to form new patterns that couple past and future in interesting ways. Esmé's hope is that people from all walks of life might locate familiar and sustaining imagery in her work and thereby enter into the visual journey of the painting. James Trilling:

> One of the biggest challenges of the maker of ornament is the creation of multiple effects; one of the biggest pleasures of ornament is seeing how the artist has made these effects coexist.
>
> Ornament—the elaboration of functionally complete objects for the sake of visual pleasure—has a unique place among the arts.[4]

A few personal observations: A lavishly glazed Italian *maiolica* platter makes palpably dignified the ritual of gathering to eat. Handmade lace adorning a shirt collar frames and decorates a person's face, much the same way petunias might border a garden. A hand-carved doorframe signals a significant threshold. Such elaborations on form do not dispute the fact that a platter must still hold food, a carpet must cover the floor, and a door must open and close. But the ornamentation elevates the importance of the otherwise mundane. There is no innate beauty to washing a dish, but the beautification of that dish elevates this otherwise humble experience.

As a potter, the space I create is tangible. Hands, lips, food, and soapsuds move through, across, and under the vessel forms I mold and decorate, and the forms themselves take up space. They must be given room in the world—on a counter, on a table-top, in the sink—in order to function. Decoration glorifies the useful object for the pleasure of the person who puts it to work.

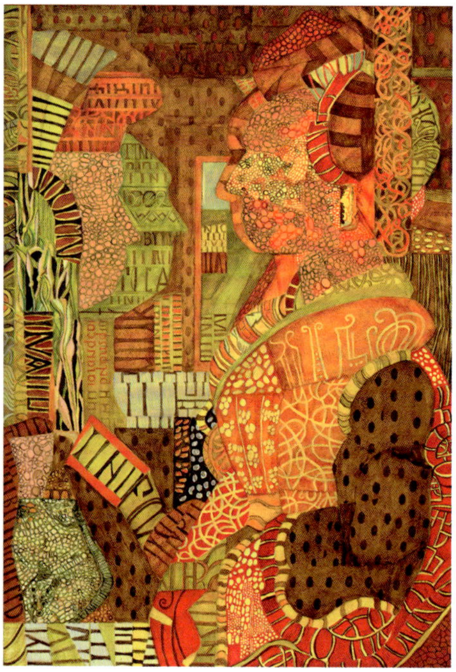

2.3. *Ritratto V*, 2008, acrylic on board.

Decoration on the surface of a pot responds to the architecture of the vessel. Like a scroll uncurling, one must follow the painting around a pot in order to fully appreciate it. The exterior surface must contend with the lip before it can visually converse with the interior surface. When the artist decorates a pot, its undulations must be respected or ignored.

Esmé evokes this world of ornament in her painting. Rather than responding to a vessel form or an architectural structure, she reacts to the blank canvas, or to the metal shape of a maple syrup bucket lid. By repeating, layering, and mirroring pattern, she creates dynamic movement and "multiple effects" of her own.

It is no wonder that Esmé also finds inspiration in medieval and early Renaissance art. The paintings she loves explore invented spaces to underscore a narrative. She has made a number of paintings and collages in response to Fra Filippo Lippi's *Woman with Man at the Window*. In *Ritratto V* (fig. 2.3), a woman and a man face each other and frame a view of a garden. During the Renaissance, the church mandated rules about what was to be included in a painting, so that its subject matter and hierarchical configuration of figures supported the doctrine of the church. The iconic figures appeared in the foreground and were usually framed with architectural details representing either the church or a nativity. This space is familiar, inviting, and safe. All of its rules are known. But what about the background—through the window, out the barn door? Here the artist was less encumbered, and unfamiliar patterns and figures inhabit this sometimes quite surreal space. The world of the imagination is much more interesting, but it is also much less safe.

Esmé's paintings and drawings often reference these Renaissance paintings, but as much for their backgrounds as for their foregrounds. She buries the figurative shape of a Renaissance woman in a world of pattern and complex narrative references, bringing the background forward. These figures have an ambiguous quality and "oscillate between decorative form and representational images."[5] Esmé distorts the familiar by creating points of restlessness in her narrative imagery, even as the figure in the painting welcomes the viewer into an intricately imaginative world. "It's my belief that through the very complexity, the sometimes compulsive process of the work, the meaning and content is found," Esmé explains. She tells her story with pattern and shape. Does she also include herself?

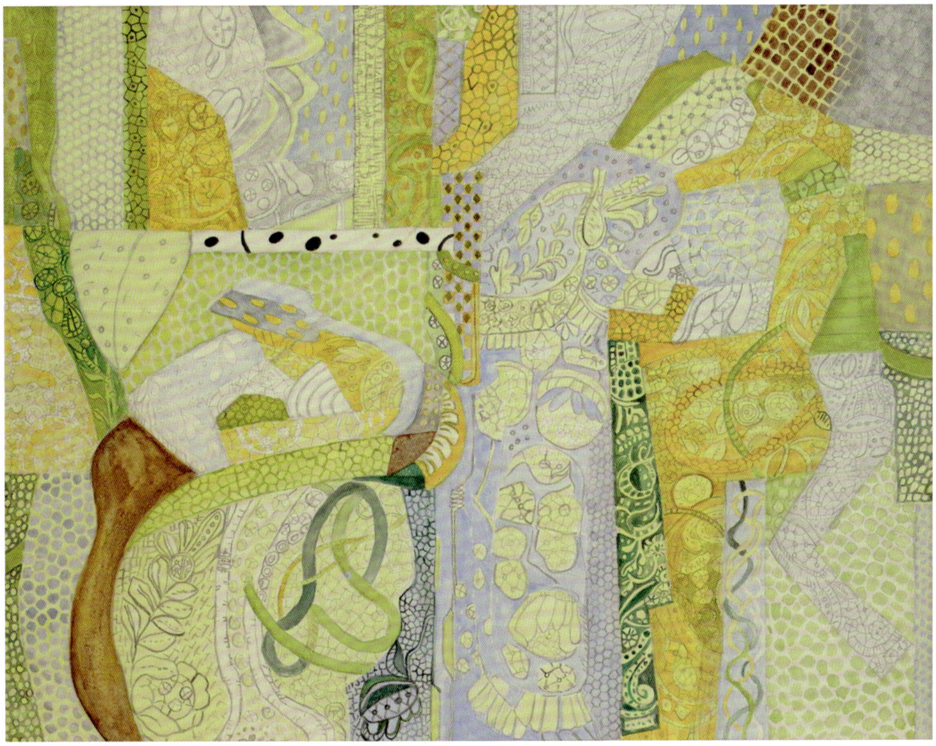

2.4. *Carrickmacross II*, 2005, acrylic on board.

Sometimes the tangled patterns obscure the figurative presence, but the subtlest suggestion of a silhouette remains. Is it the whispering figure of our gentle host? (See fig. 1.3.)

The human brain is "programmed to search for discontinuities of stimulation," Gombrich observes; we enjoy, in other words, the juxtaposition of the familiar and the unfamiliar.[6] Esmé takes advantage of this paradox in her painting *Carrickmacross II* (fig. 2.4). She derives its composition from Edouard Vuillard's *The Flowered Dress*, 1891, a favorite source (fig. 2.5). But buried in the structure of the painting is a linear design drawn in graphite that derives directly from a lace collection at the Tyrone Guthrie Centre, Annaghmakerrig, County Monaghan, Ireland, where Esmé was a resident in 2004. So how does one truly paint the space of the imagination? In Esmé's case, she juxtaposes diverse patterns like this to create complex visual interrelations that compel the viewer's involvement in trying to resolve them.

Esmé gathers visual material from all aspects of her life. Her patterns, colors, and notion of space itself are collected from a myriad of sources, some of which include illuminated manuscripts, early Renaissance painting, lace making, Italian *maiolica*, Hebraic paper cutouts, Moroccan carpet patterns, representations of micro-organisms, and gardens. Esmé chooses patterns that are at times familiar and at other times not so, and she

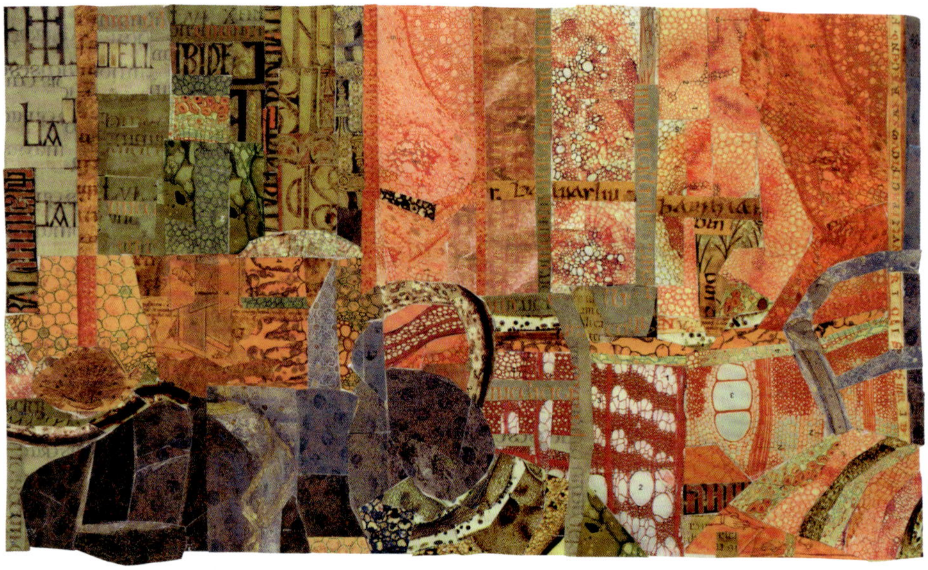

2.5. *After Vuillard II*, 2007, collage.

plays freely with color, scale, and placement to otherwise obscure them. Space in a painting arises from the abutment of diverse patterns to imply architecture or hint at a figure. In *Annaghmakerrig V*, a bent-over figure stands slightly right of the center, but the fabric is patterned and draped to entirely camouflage it (fig. 2.6). Human proportions are somewhat readable, and a vague reference to skin appears in the color of the pattern used to describe the facial area and the undergarment. Perhaps we are given a peek under the robe! The figure is bent over, as if studying, reading, or working at a wooden structure. I find myself trying to see what the figure is reading or writing, but I cannot, so next I find myself climbing under the desk, only to discover that there is no desk at all! It has given way to another pattern evoking twisted wooden boards. These disordered slats may represent an invention that is being conjured up in the mind of the figure. To the left, a window appears open to the starry night sky. The stars are repeated above the figure's head and on her robe, encircling her body entirely. She is immersed in her imagination. To the lower rear of the figure is a knotted pattern. This area of the painting is like a darkened bin, full of discarded ideas. A honeycomb pattern encircles the whole scene. Like a bee, the figure is working away in her hive. Fractured pieces of text are dispersed throughout the painting, referencing sacred writings from some personal spiritual quest. They are fragments representing pieces of knowledge gained or rules broken. Like the background of a Renaissance icon painting or the *maiolica* tile with the female torso that first inspired Esmé's use of the silhouette (fig. 2.7), her imagination unfurls on the picture plane. She tells her story through pattern and shape.

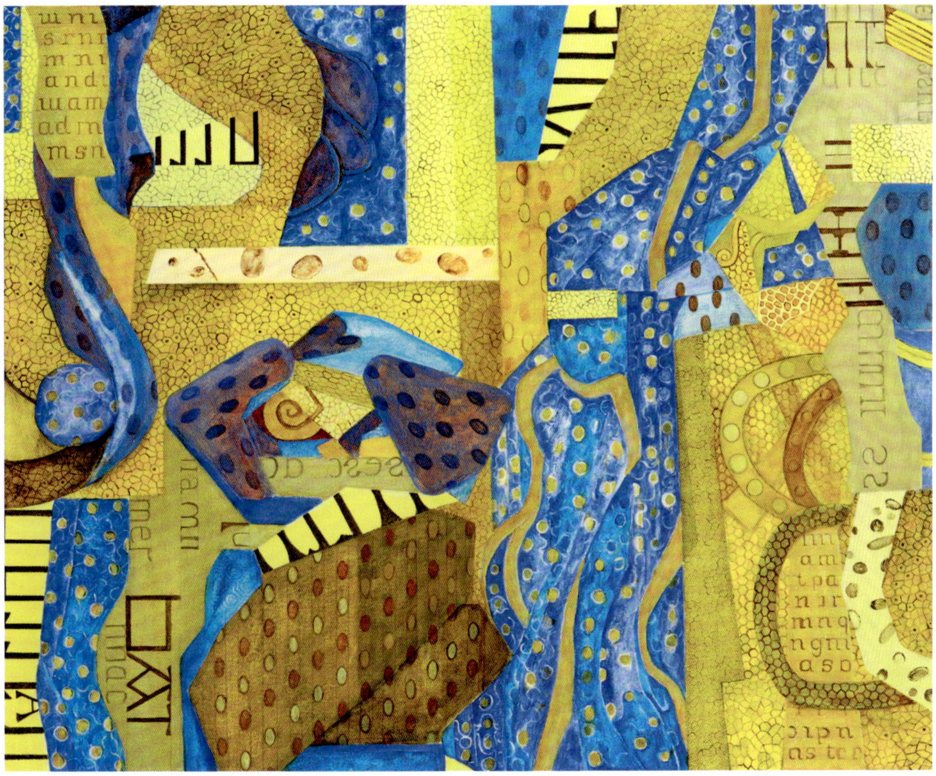

2.6. *Annaghmakerrig V,* 2005, acrylic on canvas. Photography by Hathorne/Olson.

Esmé encountered many of the traditional patterns in her paintings during travels to Ireland, Italy, England, and Morocco, where she studied the native decorative art traditions of these places. During a recent trip to Morocco, Esmé camped in the Sahara desert and worked in the Fes Pottery Cooperative. She experienced the desert culture of the Imazaghen people and its translation into woven textiles, as well as a decorative mosaic tile tradition called *zellij* (fig. 2.8). It is difficult to imagine an art form that uses a more complex and compulsive technique than this. Perfect, geometric, fingernail-sized tiles are hand chiseled from four-inch-by-four-inch handmade glazed tiles. The pieces are chiseled for a second time in order to bevel their backsides. Then, thousands of these tiles are laid face down by hand in a precise geometric grid to create an endlessly complex yet unseen surface that is in turn fixed in concrete. Suzannah Clarke writes:

> The Arabs were desert people and found the emptiness frightening. So they created a way to formally control the space. The French philosopher Pascal said that when he saw the sky and the stars it made him anxious, so he believed in God. Man needs something to measure by. In Fassi houses, symmetry is used in a way of making the

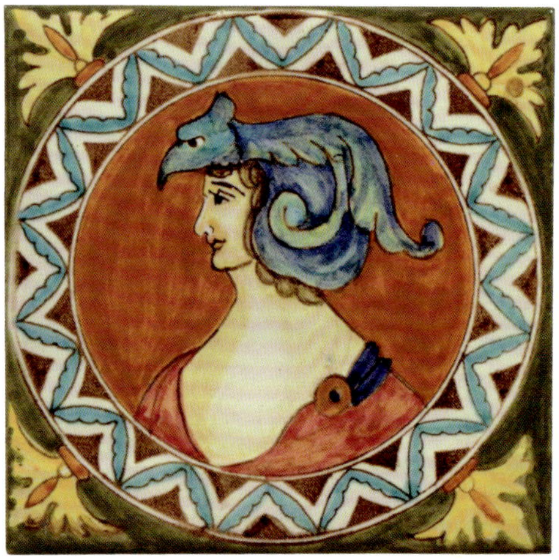

2.7. Ceramic *maiolica* tile.
Collection of the artist.

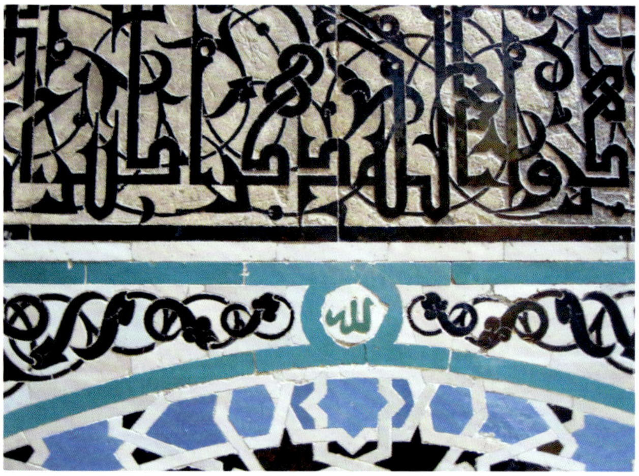

2.8. Detail of Moroccan *zellij* tile.
Photography by Esmé Thompson.

space intelligible, based around the square or rectangle. *Zellij* is like a metaphysical science, used to make measurable space.[7]

Esmé expresses a kinship to the endlessly articulated and patterned space of *zellij* in her own intensely decorated surfaces. Her most recent installation, *Djellabah*, is a direct response to the carpets and patterned mosaics she experienced in Morocco. It is composed of fifty-seven metal panels painted with elaborate patterns. The panel patterns first respond to the contour of the modular shape and then are repeated, reflected, and mirrored on other panels across the wall. The result is a complex, multi-layered space of woven color, shape, and mark. It represents possibility; it embodies change (fig. 2.9). Rather than seeking answers or making didactic statements, Esmé discovers as she goes and then invites her viewers on the journey. Her painting process and the work itself draws us into her spaces like a gardener draws people through her garden. Carefully positioning intermittent references to the familiar, she lures the viewer into the work of discovering the new in her painted environments. Narratives are only quietly implied, and clues are subtle at best. Esmé herself observes:

> I have a life-long interest in painting as an experience or environment. The patterns and shapes that repeat throughout my work form an internal dynamic of cross-referenced imagery and a sense of mutability and shifting possibilities for viewing. These repeated images are cyclical and cumulative, rather than a linear narrative. The painting becomes a journey that continues to unfold, reminiscent of an ongoing pattern of organic growth.

Esmé assimilates the work of the gardener in her paintings. Her brushstrokes alight here and there across the canvas, pollinating the seen and the unseen in her work, as she celebrates the tangible world that is before us and the mysterious realm hidden beneath. As we journey through the "landscape" of her paintings, we are surprised to discover ourselves to be very much at home.

NOTES

1. Vita Sackville-West, quoted in Caroline Seebohm and Christopher Simon Sykes, *Private Gardens* (New York: Clarkson N. Potter, Inc., 1989), vii.
2. Robert Taylor, "Pictures You Can Walk through at Exeter," *Boston Sunday Globe*, September 30, 1984.
3. See Lucy Lippard, "The Pink Glass Swan: Upward and Downward Mobility in the Art World," *Heresies* 1, no. 1 (1977): 84.
4. James Trilling, *The Language of Ornament* (London: Thames and Hudson, 2001), 6, 51.
5. E. H. Gombrich, *The Sense of Order* (London: Phaidon Press, 1979), 256.
6. Ibid., 121.
7. Suzannah Clarke, *A House in Fez* (New York, Pocket Books, 2007), 123.

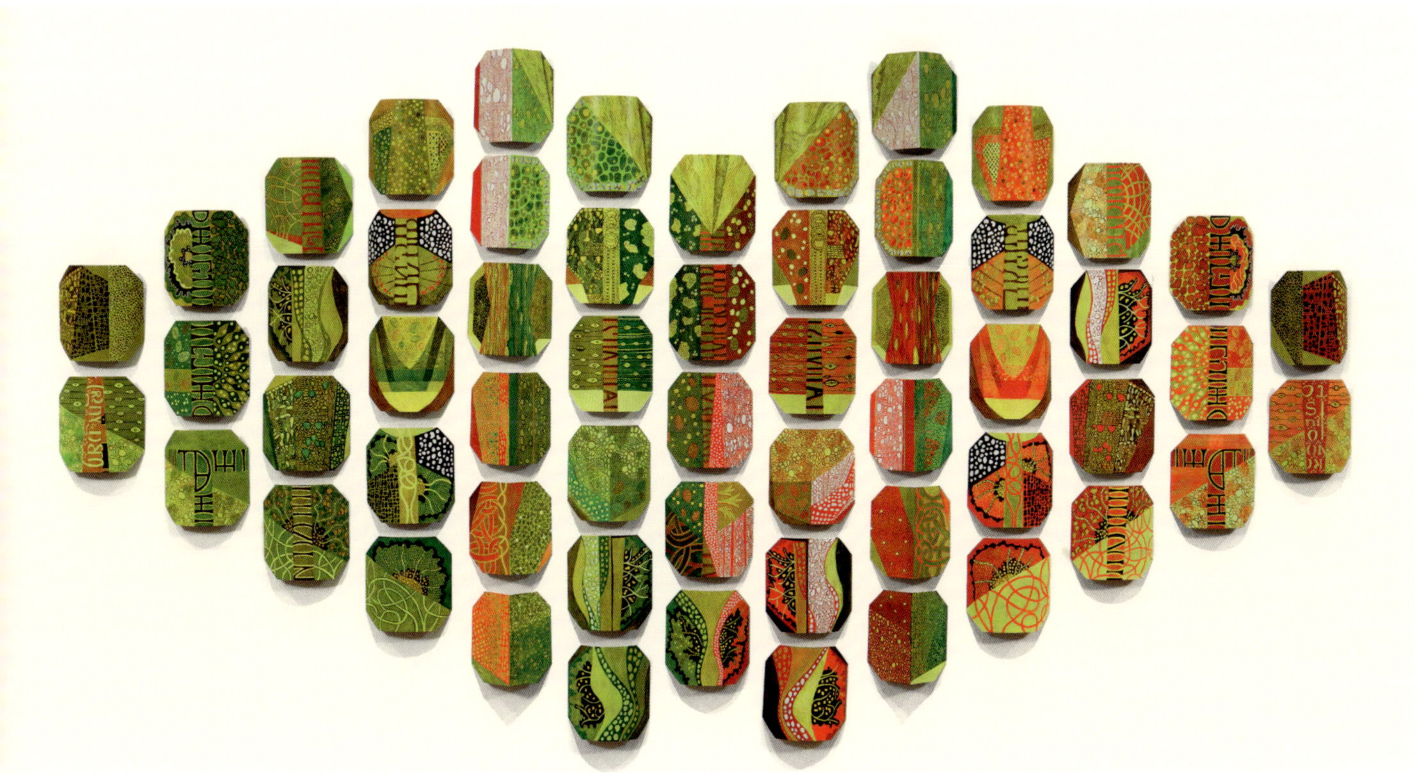

2.9. *Djellaba*, 2010, fifty-seven-piece installation, acrylic on metal, 94 x 194 x 3 inches.

Plates

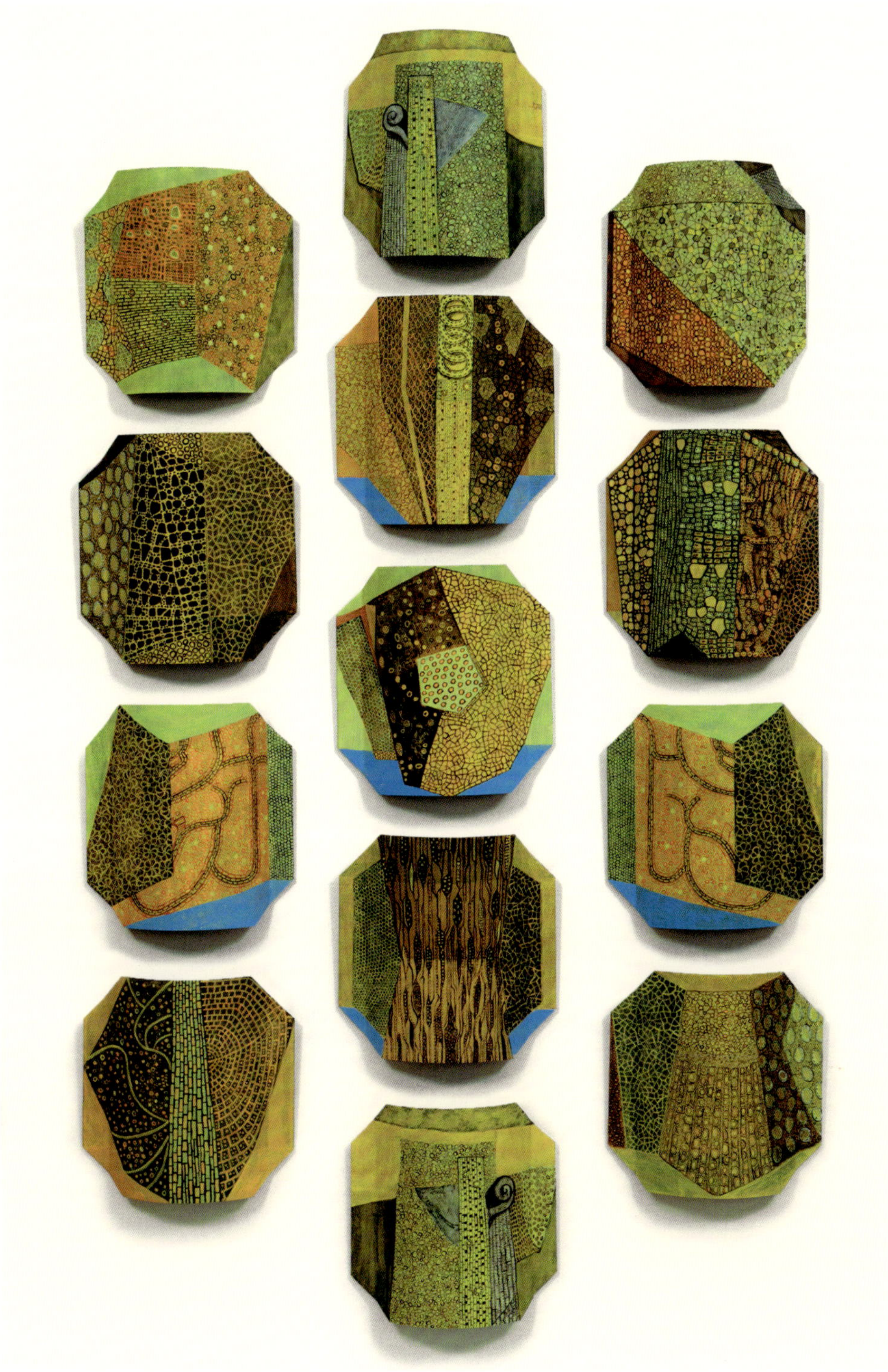

1. *Beatus II,* 2003, thirteen-piece installation, acrylic on metal, 69 x 42 x 3 inches.

2. *Ornamentum I*, 2004, acrylic on canvas.

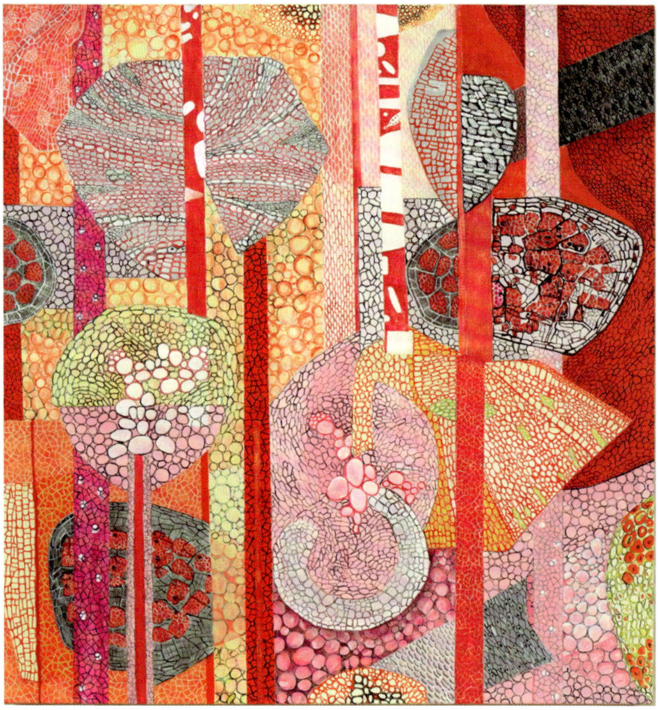

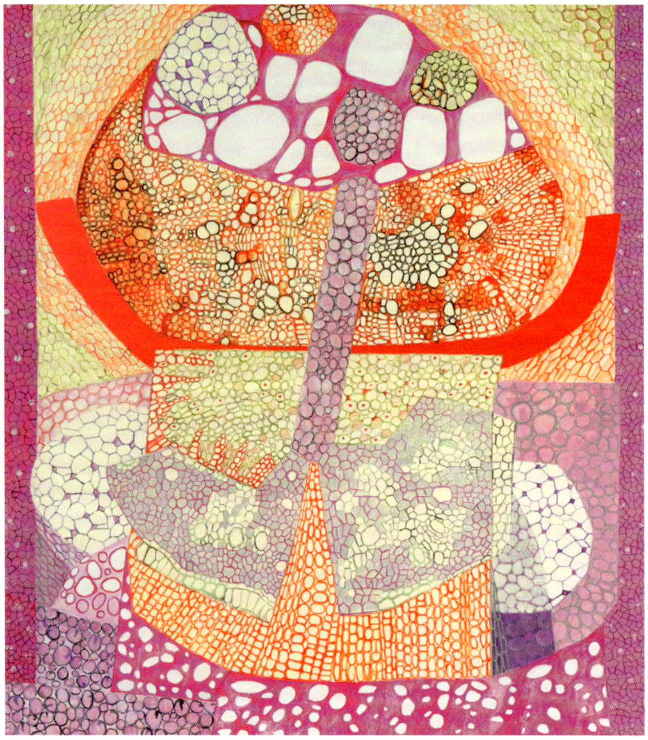

3. *Ornamentum IV*, 2005, acrylic on canvas. Photography by Hathorne/Olson

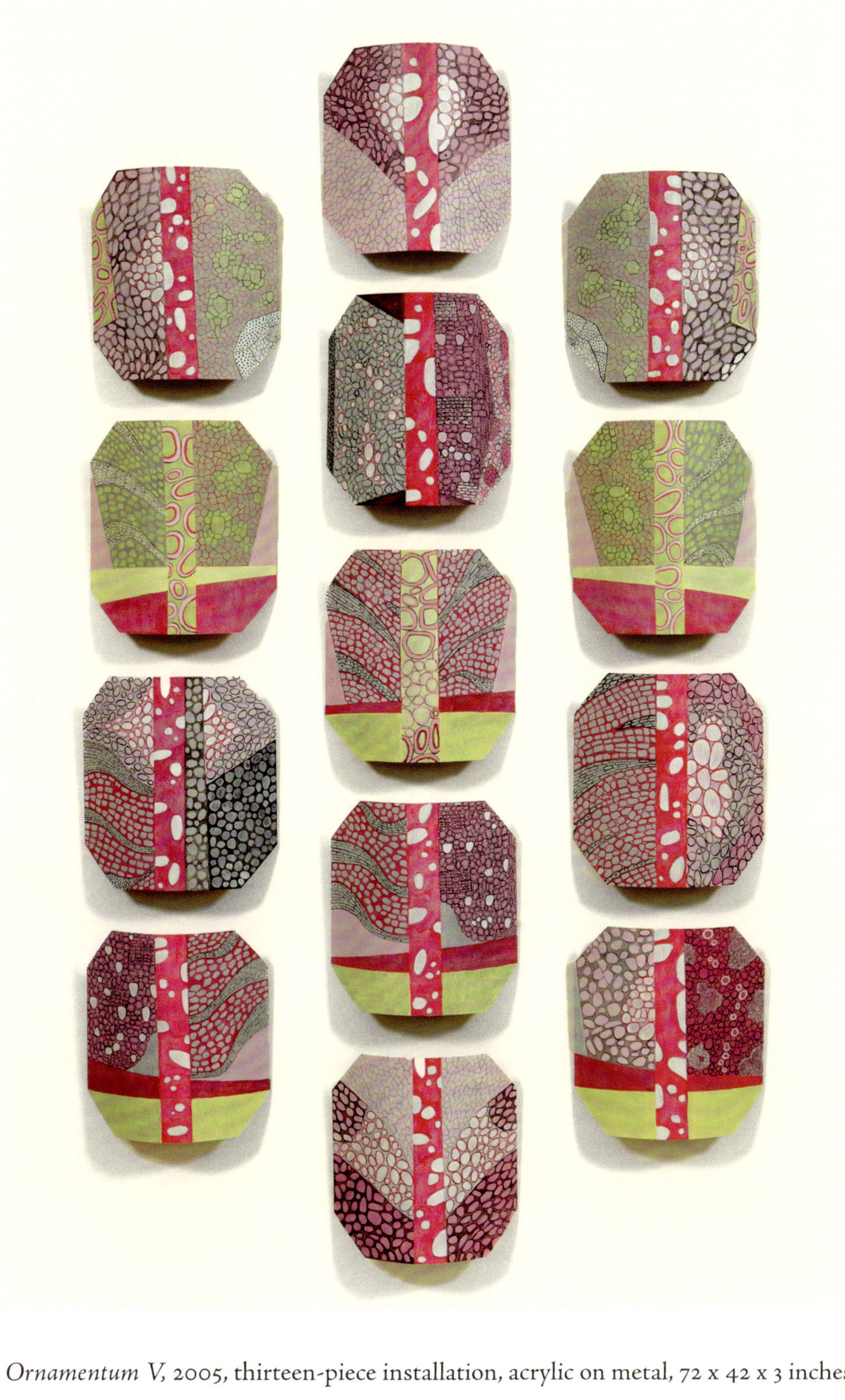

4. *Ornamentum V,* 2005, thirteen-piece installation, acrylic on metal, 72 x 42 x 3 inches.

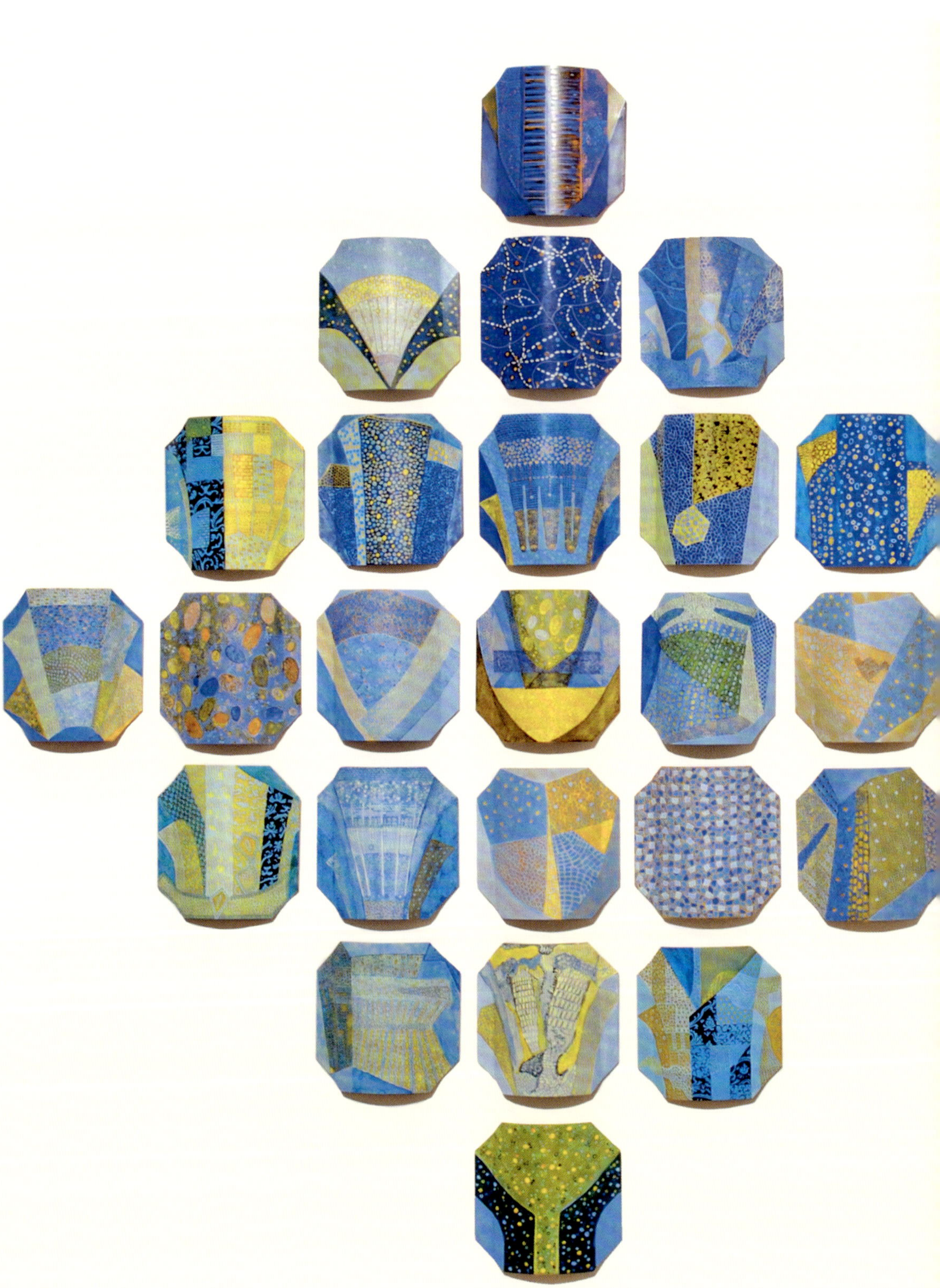

5. *Blue Divide*, 2005, forty-nine-piece installation, acrylic on metal, 94 x 194 x 3 inches.

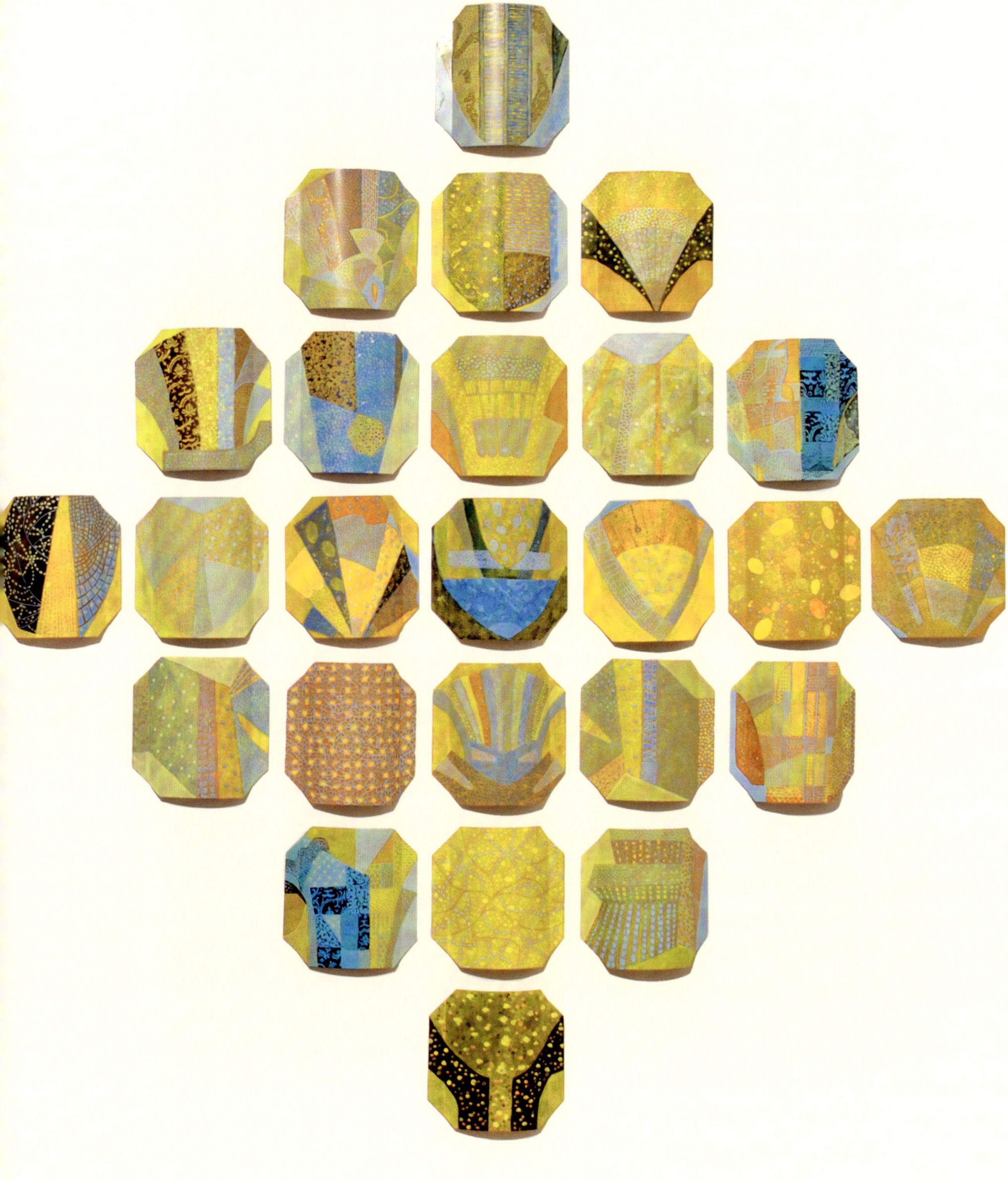

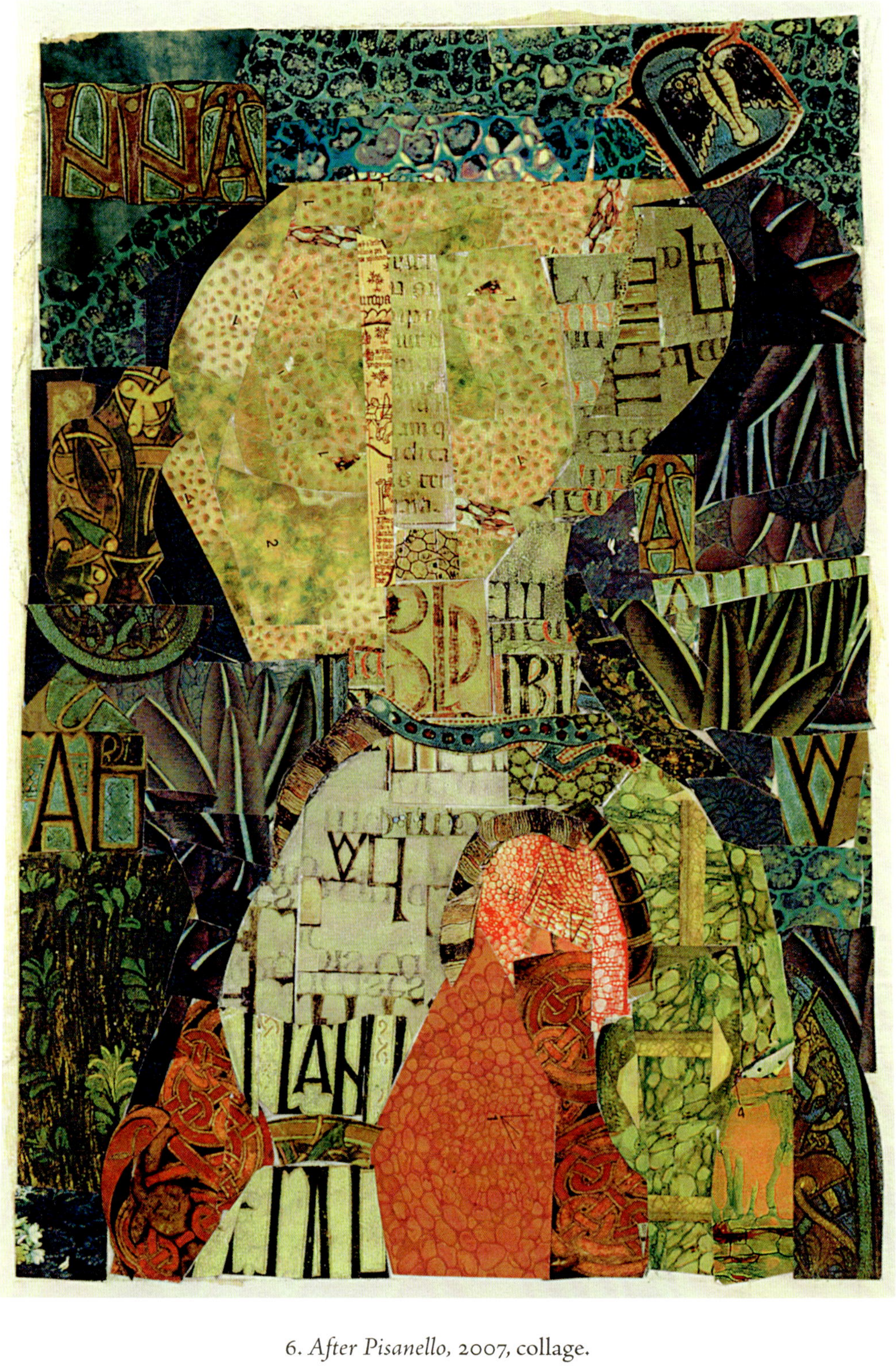

6. *After Pisanello,* 2007, collage.

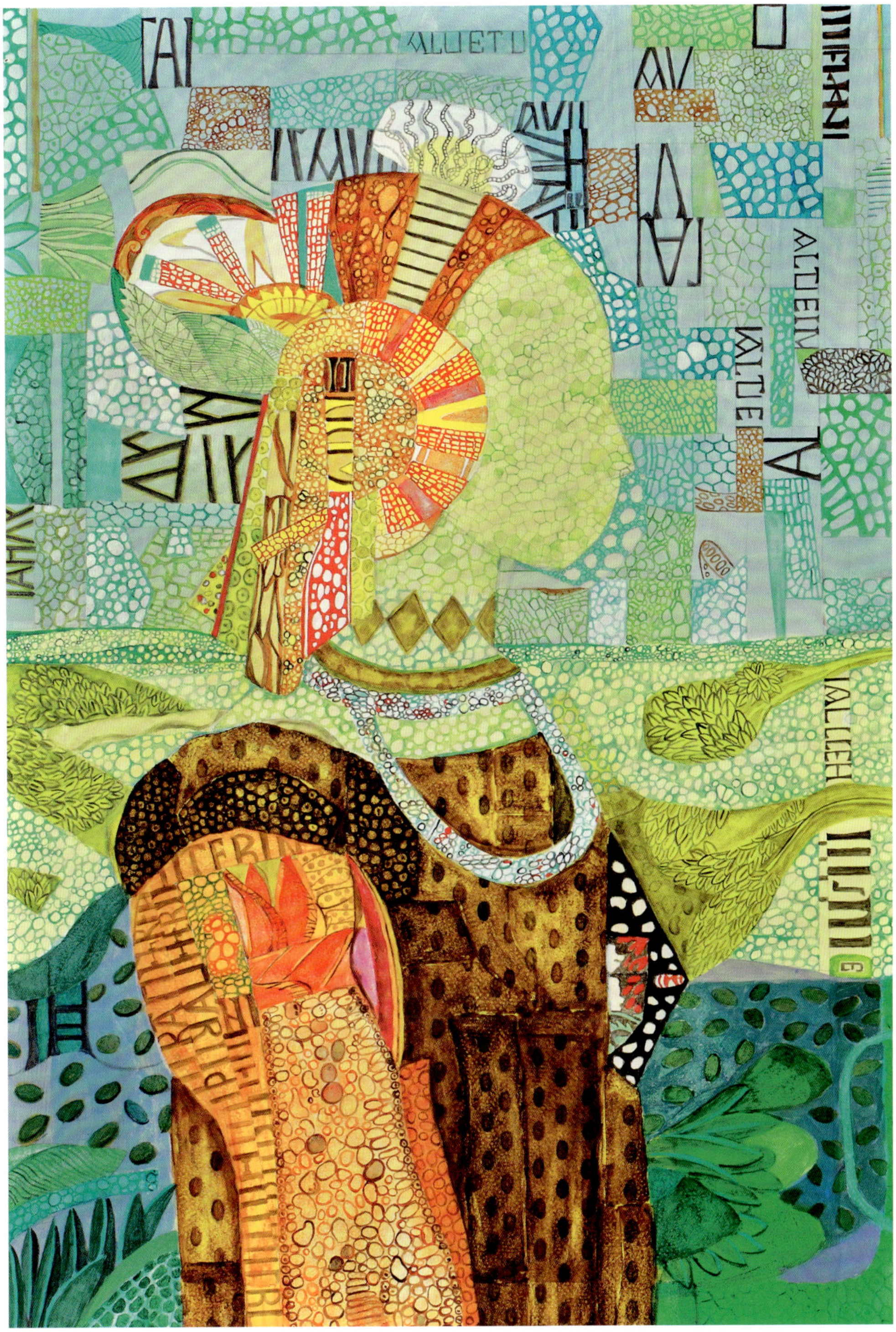

7. *Ritratto I*, 2007, acrylic on board. Photography by Hathorne/Olson.

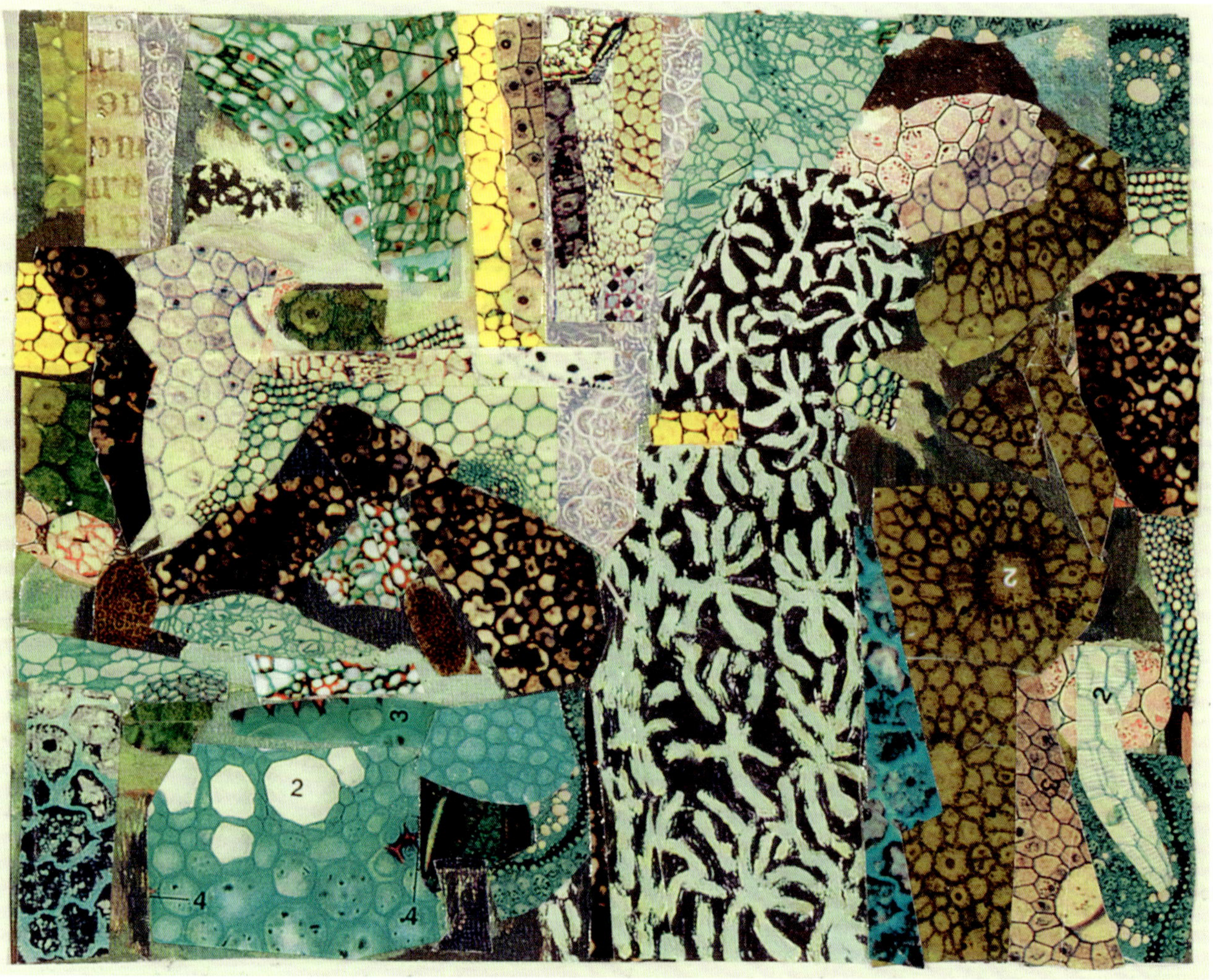

8. *After Vuillard/Annaghmakerrig*, 2004, collage.

9. Opposite: *At the Window*, 2008, collage.

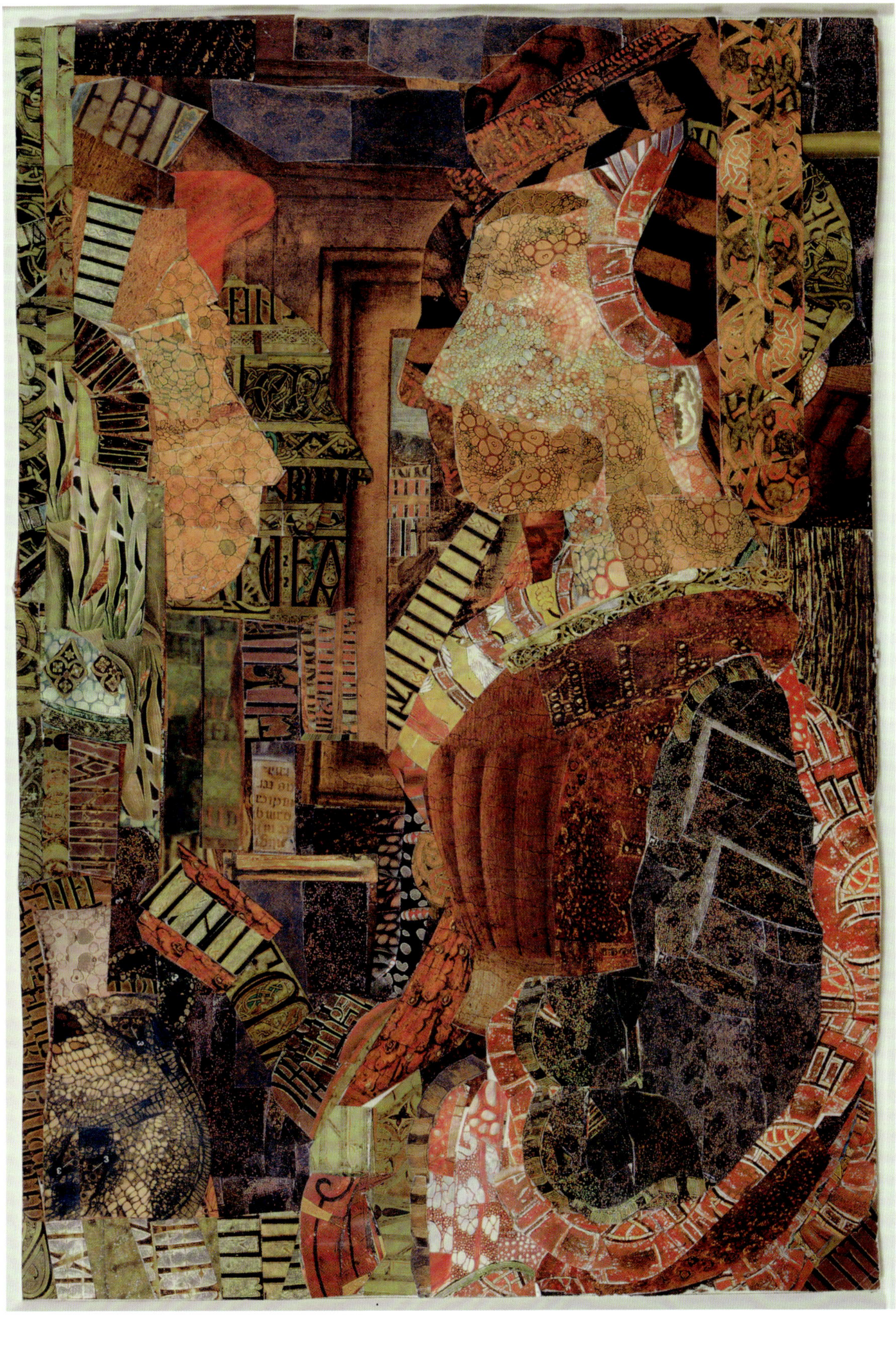

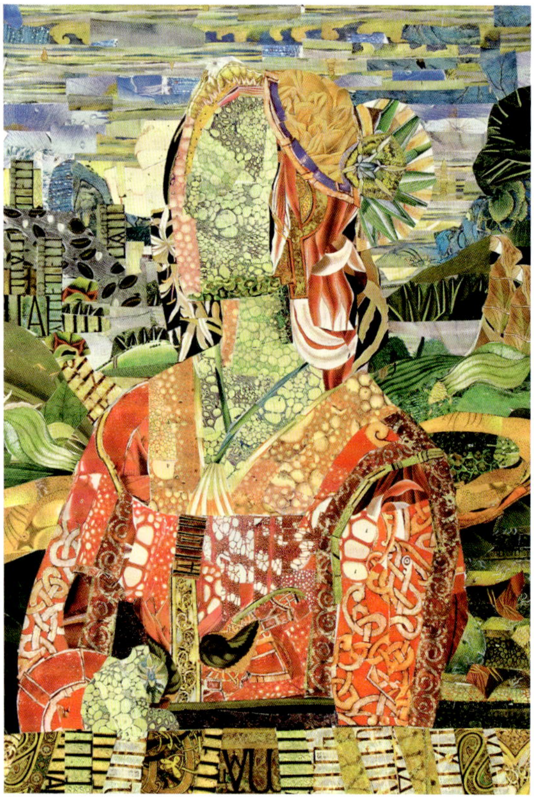

10. *Donna,* 2008, collage.

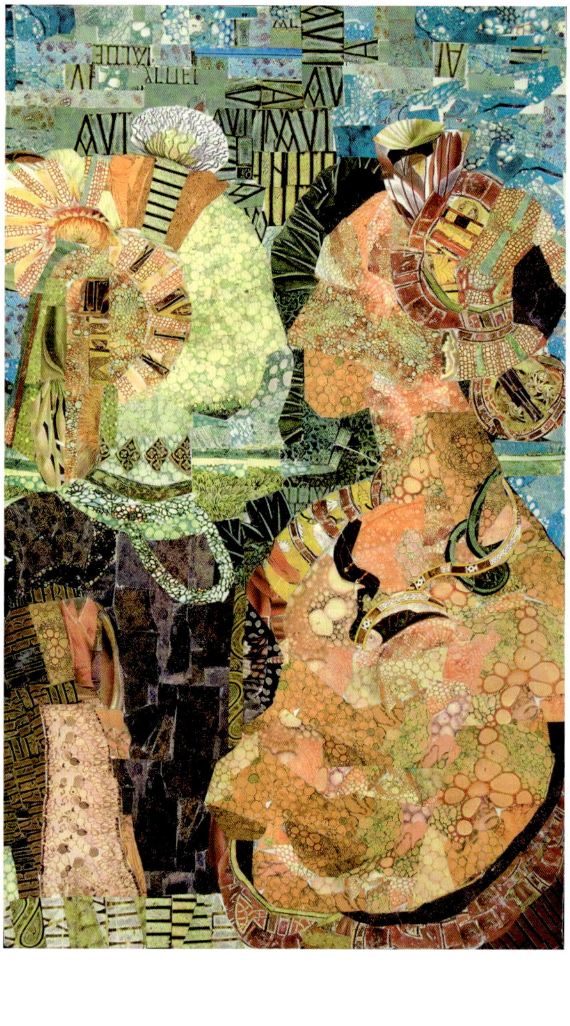

11. *Incontriamo,* 2008, collage.

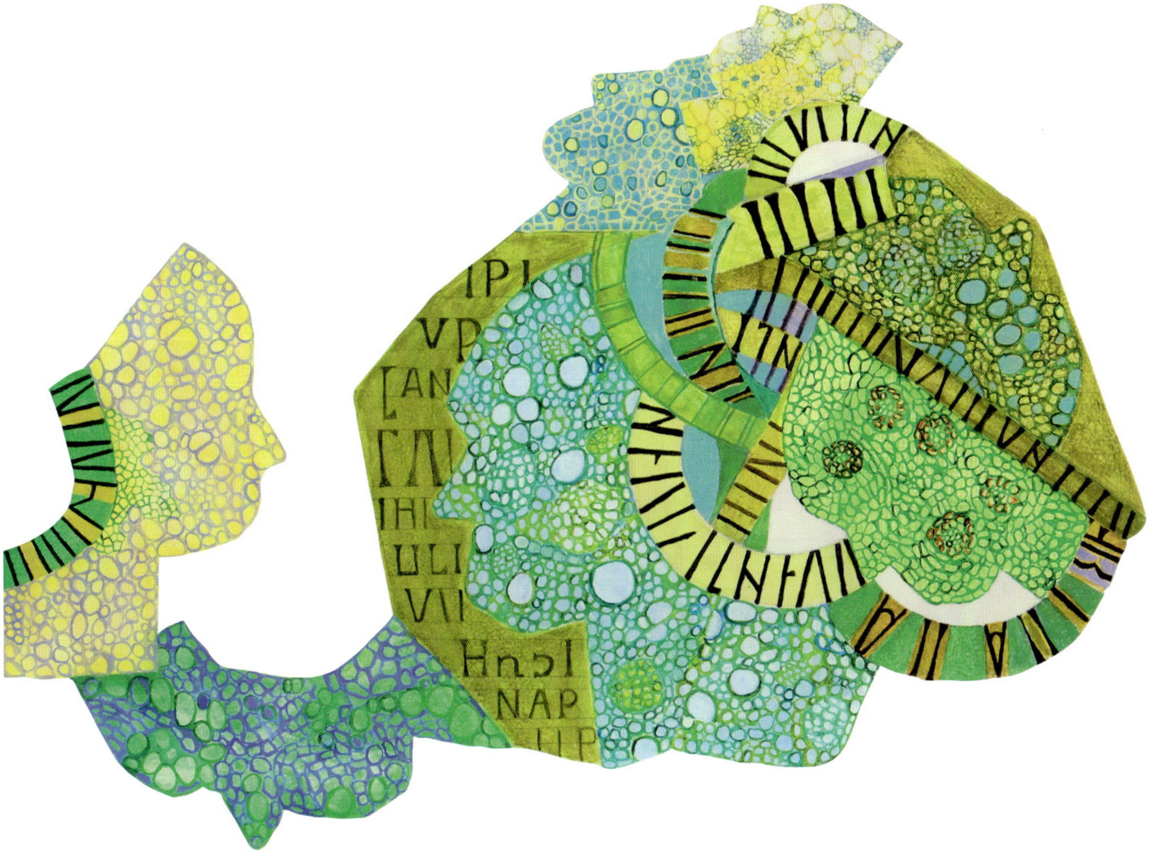

12. *Tipsy II,* 2008, acrylic and collage on board. Photography by Hathorne/Olson.

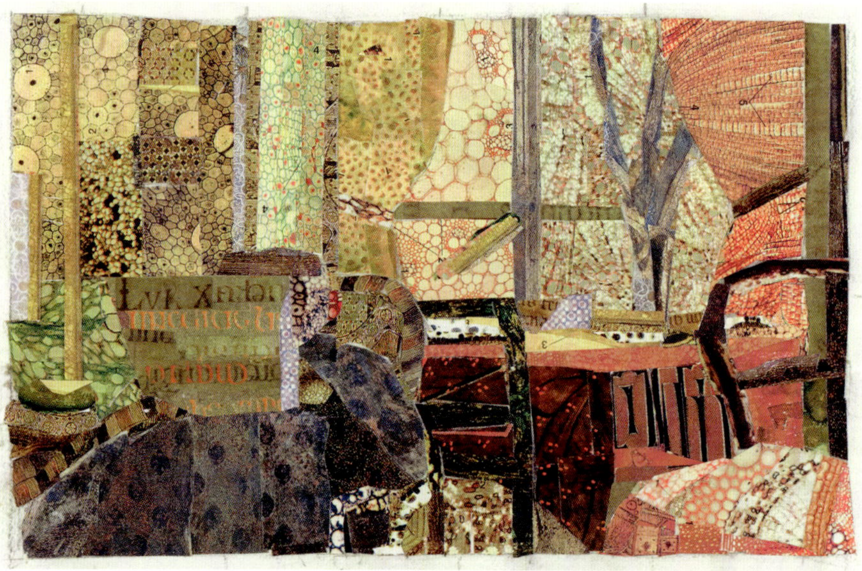

13. *After Vuillard/Lisant,* 2007, collage.

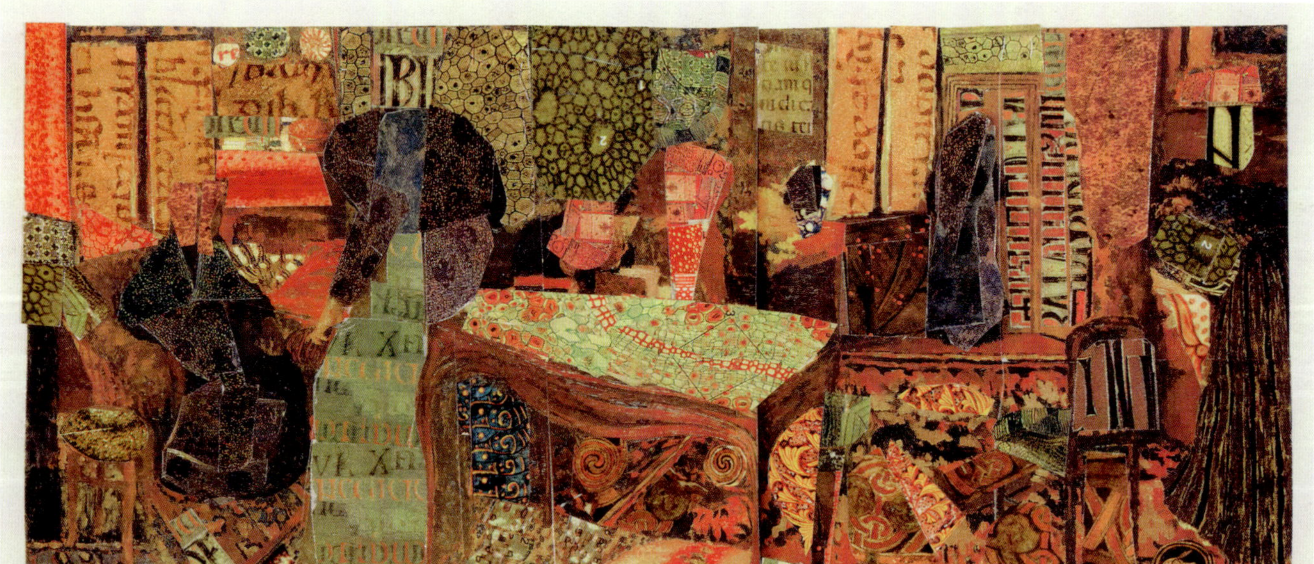

14. *After Vuillard IV,* 2007, collage.

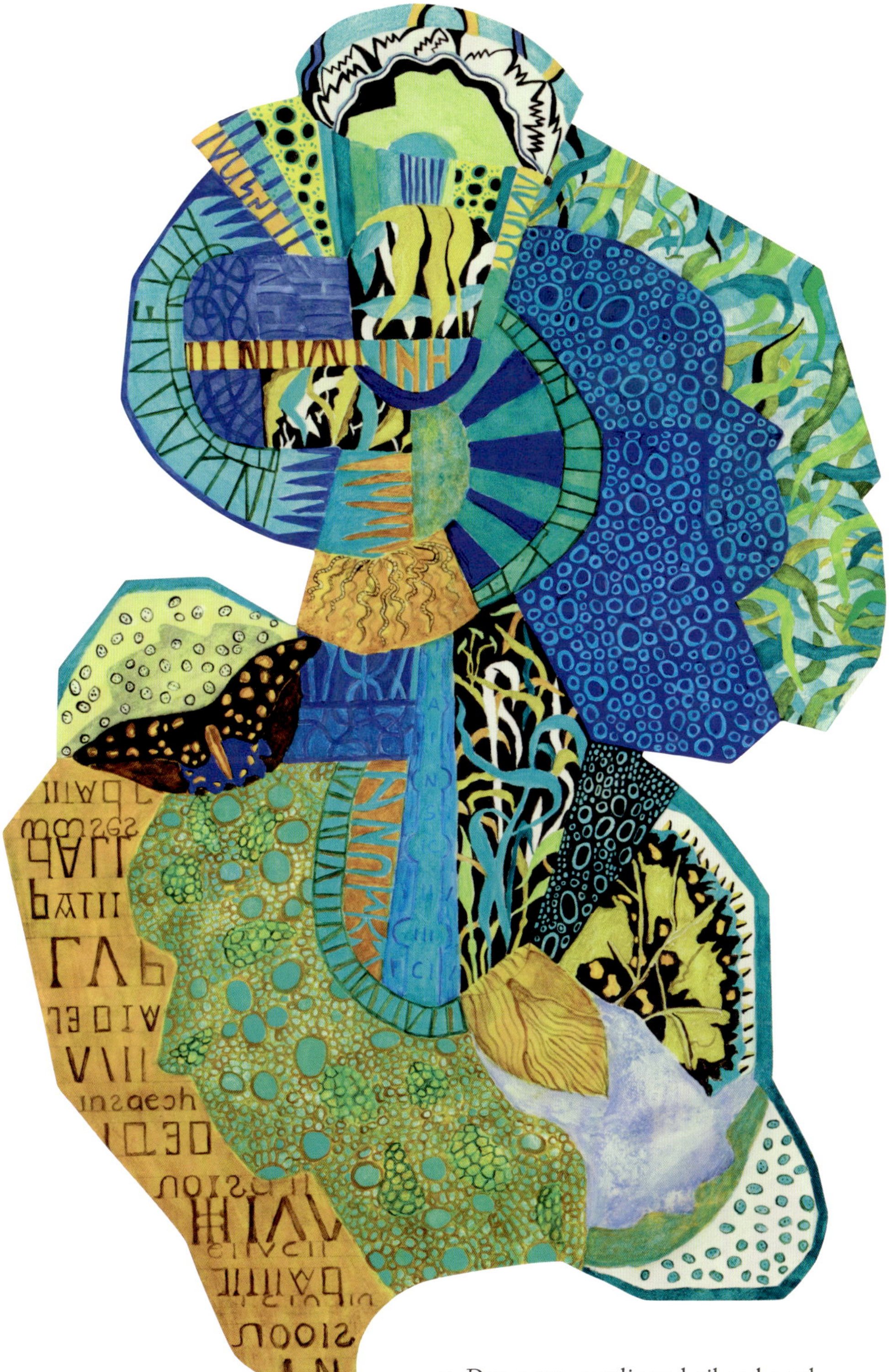

15. *Duo*, 2010, acrylic and oil on board.

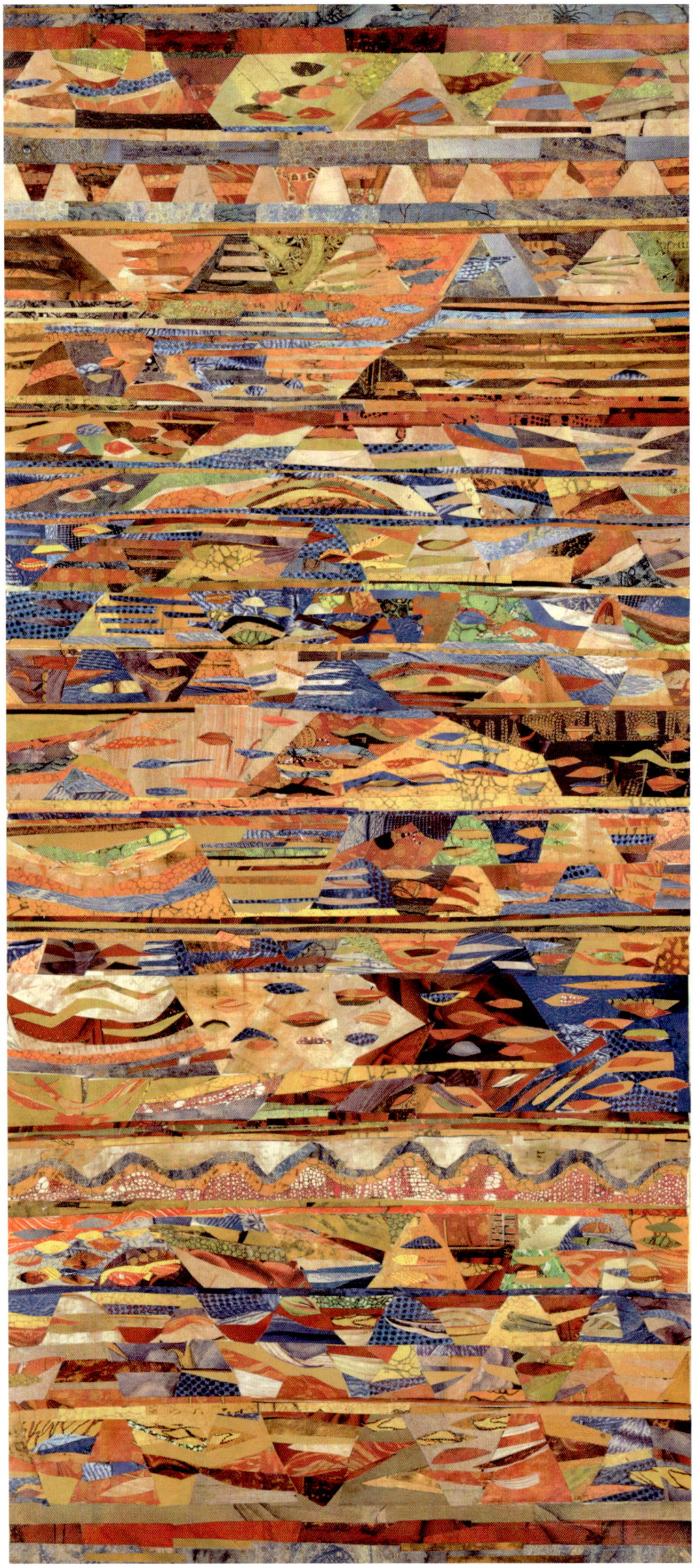

16. Opposite: *Tit 'n-teskourt,* 2010, collage.

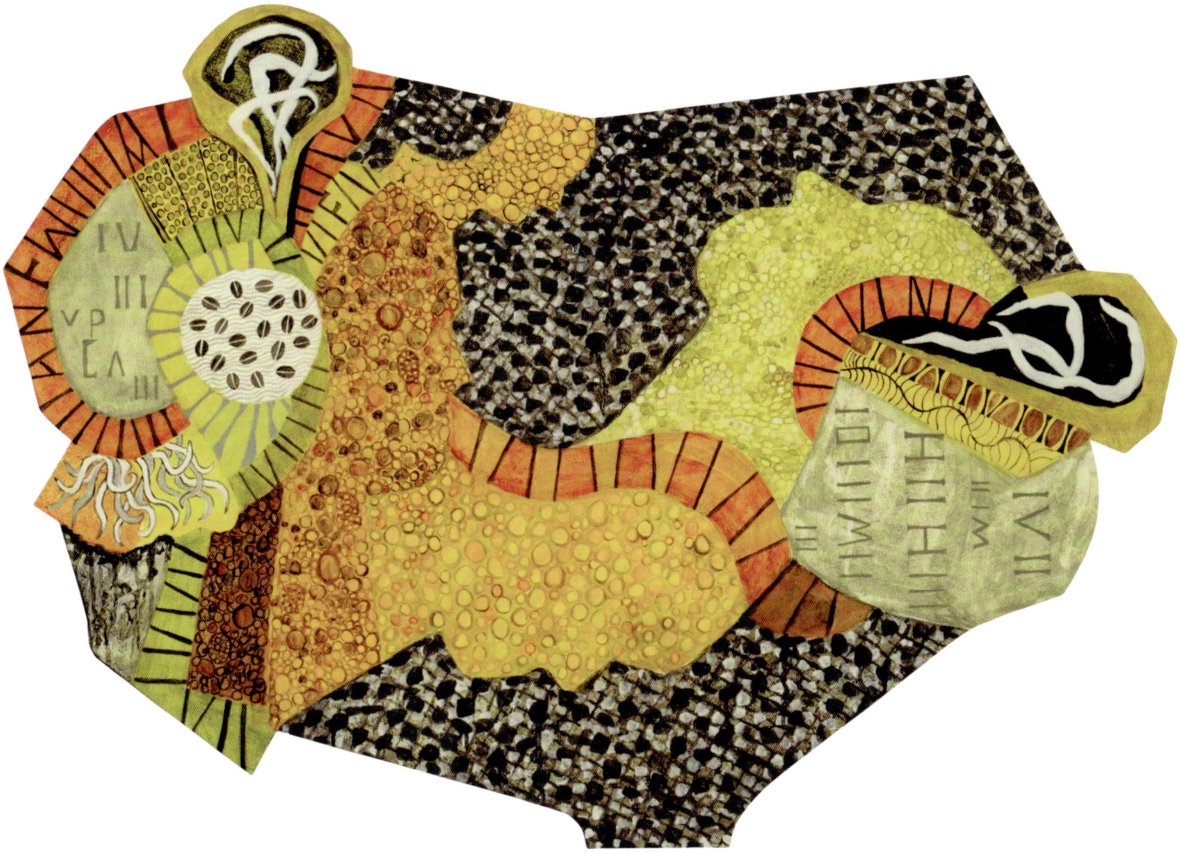

17. *Trio IV,* 2010, acrylic and oil on board.

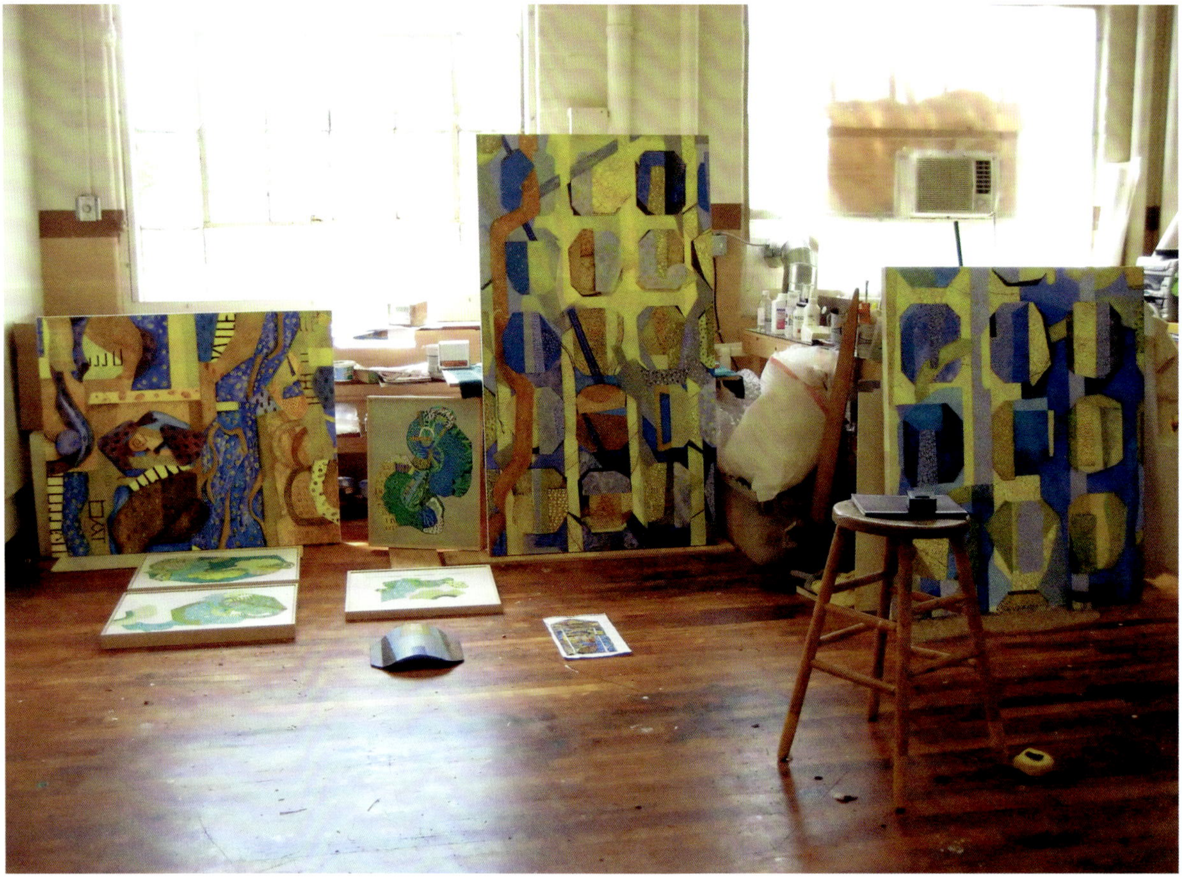

Esmé Thompson's Lebanon studio. Photography by Patrick Dunfey.

3

A Conversation with Esmé Thompson

BRIAN KENNEDY

Based on an interview on August 5, 2010, in Thompson's studio in Lebanon, New Hampshire.

BRIAN KENNEDY: You're from California.

ESMÉ THOMPSON: Yes, from La Jolla.

BK: What was it like being a Californian coming to New England?

ET: I had a long journey to get here, because I went to college in Spokane, Washington, so I lived in Washington State for ten years. I never felt like I really "fit in" in California, so it was like I was an escapee. I loved Washington State. After I completed an English degree in college, I moved back to Spokane, and like all English majors, I was waitressing. I started getting interested in art at the Spokane Studio School. Ben Moss started that school with some colleagues, and it was perfect for me because it wasn't a typical academic structure. It was just a group of artists making a space work. And from when I was twenty-four on, I was totally obsessed with making art. I moved east to continue my education first at University of Iowa and then at Yale. Then I got a job at Dartmouth, and for about the first twenty years I was a Dartmouth, I always thought I wanted to be in New York, and in the last ten years, I've sort of come to terms with living in New England. I like being here now, but for a long time I thought I had to be in New York. It's isolating to live up here, for an artist. It's not easy to get to the city.

BK: Where was your family from?

ET: My grandparents on my mother's side were from Australia and Canada, and they lived in Detroit. My mom moved out to California during the Second World War to work in an airplane plant. And my father was from New York.

BK: Was it an artistic family?

ET: My father was an engineer at Convair in San Diego. I never had much contact with him. My mother didn't go to college, but she was very creative. She was always encouraging of anything that was creative as well. For whatever reason, she loved everything I ever did. So that was helpful.

BK: You said you were an English major. What course did you take that caused you to end up being a practicing artist?

ET: Well, just dropping out from society in general, and coming back to it through art.

BK: What happened to you?

ET: I was living in Washington State even after college. It was the sixties. I lived in Seattle for a while in a commune. My first husband wanted to go "back to nature." It was all these middle-class American kids who'd been raised in the suburbs who wanted to go live in the wilds. We had a child and moved out to this little cabin that was really a shack in Nespelem, Washington, on the Colville Reservation. We lived there for a winter. The snow would blow in through the cracks in the cabin wall. We really didn't know what we were doing. I was baking bread on a wood stove and boiling water to wash clothes. It was very primitive, no electricity, reading books by an oil lamp and listening to our battery-powered radio. You learn that you can live in a very simple way and be happy.

Both my mom and my stepfather were gardeners. My mother had this quirky, luscious, crazy garden full of all kinds of fig trees, lemon trees, orchids, and every kind of plant imaginable in a backyard in suburban southern California. Everything that you would love if you were a four-year-old child—you'd just be in awe in that space. So I started having gardens of my own as soon as possible. That has been something important to me that connects me with my mother. I think about things that she loved and I plant things that she loved. It just resonates through me.

When I first started painting, I was painting the way everybody else around me was painting. At the Spokane Studio School we had these tiny studios, and there'd be four of us in them and everybody was trying to paint like Bonnard. It was a revelation to me to first go to a museum and actually see what Bonnard looked like, because I thought he painted like an abstract expressionist.

BK: Can you remember where that was?

ET: I think it was at the Museum of Art in Chicago. I saw my first Bonnard and realized, "Oh, well, paintings don't have to be built up, they can have that different kind of touch." Still, to this day, I look at Bonnard and Vuillard. Vuillard, especially, has been a big influence on my work. I saw a big Vuillard show up in Montreal, and I was knocked out by that.

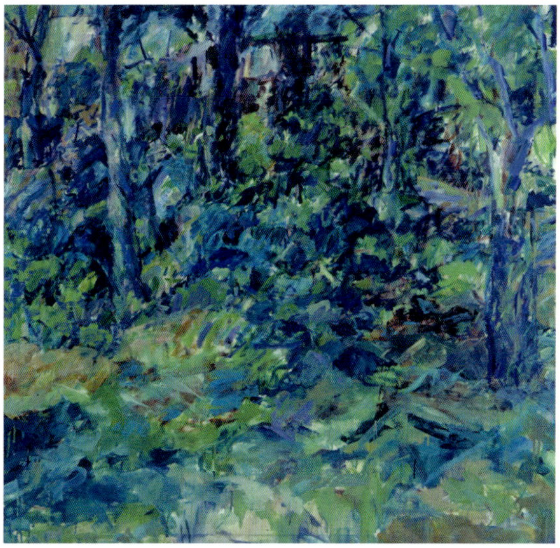

3.1. *Norfolk*, 1975, oil on canvas.
Photography by Esmé Thompson.

BK: Tell me about your teachers. You mentioned Vuillard and Bonnard, but tell me about others, the artists and the teachers who've influenced you?

ET: Ben Moss was a big influence and a big supporter. He did a lot for his students. He set up a board of trustees at the Spokane Studio School and, very wisely, invited people from the New York Studio School and from Yale. Robert Reed, who taught at Yale, ran Yale Norfolk. I found this out so many years later—that Reed was making an effort to find students from schools that weren't for the privileged, that weren't the "Ivies," and so I think our school in Spokane, which was run on a shoestring, was really interesting and appealing to him. Going to Yale Norfolk was a huge break for me, because then I studied with Louis Finkelstein. I had been doing these kind of abstract expressionist paintings, but I didn't have any idea what I was doing. I was looking at de Kooning and trying to figure him out. So much of what I had done has been based on books, because I hadn't lived near museums. Louis took us out into nature to paint. I was a single mom, living on welfare and working as a waitress to get by. My parents took my daughter, and I had the summer at Yale Norfolk. I had never known what it was like to have all that time to work, so I worked harder than anybody. I did these great big landscape paintings. I dragged the easel out into the landscape [fig. 3.1] and worked on huge canvases. I had this feeling that instead of wanting to do a landscape as a vista, I wanted to do a landscape that I felt like I was inside of, which is relevant to everything else I've ever done.

I remember where I was when I got accepted to Yale. I was in Iowa, on the stairway, in this concrete-block apartment building where I was living. It was riddled with cockroaches. And a letter came from Yale. I opened it on the stairway and it was an acceptance. It made a big difference for me. Because then I went and I studied at Yale with Elizabeth Murray, John Walker, Al Held, Lester Johnson, and Bernie Chaet. I learned so much; I was like a sponge. At that point in my life, I was just absorbing so much information.

BK: Did you go to art history courses?

ET: I've only had a few art history courses. I had a course on Monet at Yale. We talked about Monet's series and the professor's big discovery was that Monet dragged his brush over the rough surface to make another layer of color. You know it's so obvious to anybody that paints.

BK: The reason I asked the question about art history is that it seems to me in your work that there's a huge interest in artistic styles from around the world. It's very obvious that you're hugely interested in what's happening in lots of different places.

ET: Yes, but the art history I've responded to has been from my travels and my own research, not from any course I took. And if you look at the work that I'm doing now, there's an interest in the crafts. I think the Craft and Pattern movement and the feminist movement in the seventies really laid the foundation for trying to make art non-hierarchical. I taught at the Chautauqua Institution, at the point when the program had every kind of area, from clay to glass to metalworking to papermaking to weaving, and I started to realize that my background had been very narrow in the sense of being mostly based in painting, not even sculpture. I got very interested in the kinds of craft and decorative art that goes on across the world. So what I'm interested in when I travel is what people are making in that area. I remember I was in Dingle, Ireland. It was a little lace-making museum, and there was a young woman who was making a piece of lace. It was like the most beautiful drawing I had ever seen. I also began to connect with manuscripts, the text in manuscripts; it really resonated with me in terms of drawing or mark-making. A fragment could become a pattern [see fig. 2.5].

BK: You mentioned pattern and decoration. Did you feel enabled or facilitated by the feminist movement?

ET: Yes. One thing that was going on in the seventies was that artists were working with any kind of material. There was a period in the art world that you couldn't make a lot of money, so someone like Judy Pfaff could make these wild environments from stuff she found on New York City's Canal Street in the plastic store and in the hardware store. Charles Simonds could make these little cities that were in the cracks of the sidewalk and then got destroyed. Memory played a big part in the experience of this work, because it only existed for a brief time. Eventually those artists had to figure out how to make something they could sell, though, or else they had to teach. So yes, those artists, mainly women, opened up the context of what art could be made from.

I am not naïve at all about what it's like for a woman in the arts versus what it's like for a man. But I don't really want to bring anger and resentment into my studio, and I don't feel the need to make a political statement with my work. I feel that making art is a political act, especially these days. I strongly feel the value of making things, things that reflect your personality within the context of your culture. Everything else in our society seems to be based on making money. I know there's a lot of money to be made by making art, but most of the artists I know don't make money. Most of the artists I know are making art because they feel compelled to engage in this activity, this process that is really a journey of a lifetime. That's what it feels like to me. I think my political act is trying to make work that's more accessible, that isn't condescending. There may be a dialogue to go along with it that references other things, but I think I make work that is more available to people that don't have a lot of art education. This is particularly true with the installations I've done, from the very beginning when I did those hanging screens to my current metal pieces; I found that people could look at them in a lot of ways and bring something of themselves to them. That is important to me.

BK: Can you talk a little bit about your relationship with space? I mean it's obviously been a preoccupation, but how has it changed? Some people work from the flat to the room installation, and you were working in the room installation and then maybe moving toward the flat.

ET: I think I was interested in it from the very beginning, when I was doing landscape painting, trying to get paintings that felt like they were surrounding me, and drawings that didn't have a center point of focus—so I was inside of them. And then I saw the *Planar Dimensions* exhibition at the Guggenheim Museum. This exhibition included Russian constructivist and cubist artists who did paintings that moved off the wall. I was graduating from Yale, and I went to Italy. I made a point of going to see paintings that you could only see in the site rather than going to museums. It was a time when people were doing site-specific work. I went to the Romanesque chapel of San Pietro al Monte in Civate, where you had to hike two hours to get to this church up on the top of a mountain. It was a tiny little chapel, and the interior was covered with paintings. It had a main painting of

St. Michael and the Dragon, but it had paintings on the walls all around it [fig. 3.2]. It felt that part of the experience was the journey to get there, the inaccessibility of it. Part of it was being out of breath and walking into this cool, dark space. It wasn't lit like a museum. It was like you were back in time, in another space. And the painting, well, you were part of it.

So when I came back, I started to explore ways to make that happen, and I tried a bunch of things that weren't too successful, like dioramas. They had a floor piece and then three layers. I found this material called Flexipane that they use to make windows on pigpens and things like that. So I'd get it at the hardware store and I found ways to make hanging screens out of it. I would create installations that had, sometimes, hundreds of these screens, and they would be hung to form pathways so that you could go inside of them. I did a piece at Phillips Exeter Academy where they have four adjacent galleries, and they could change the light in four different ways with a combination of screens, lights, and skylights [see fig. 2.2]. I was influenced by Jennifer Bartlett's *In the Garden,* and I had just begun gardening myself. I did four seasons in my garden at Exeter—the first was spring, then summer, and autumn, and winter. After the first room, the light was screened

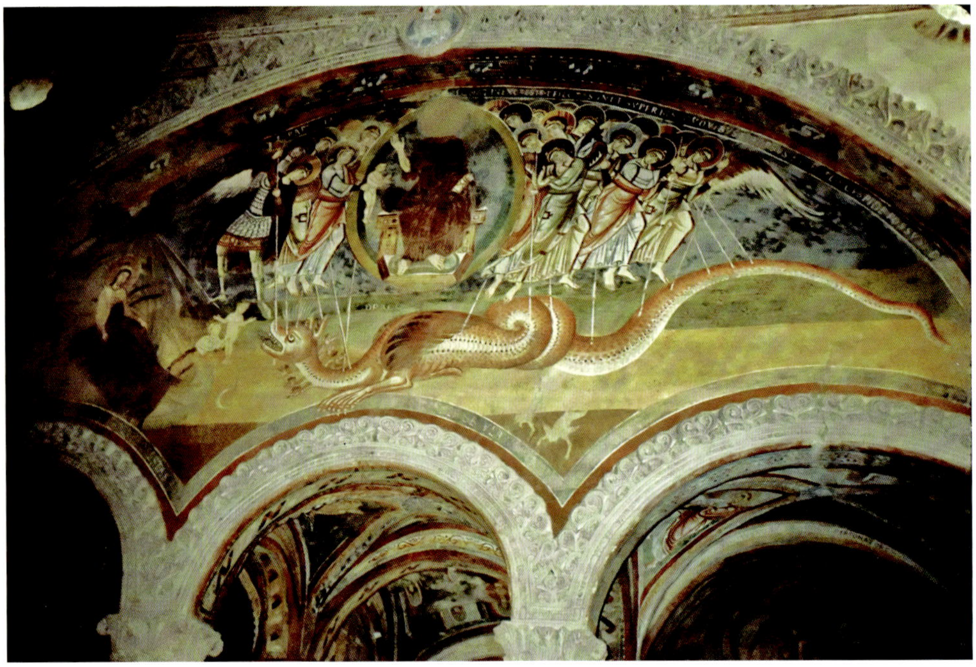

3.2. *Apse of San Pietro al Monte,* late twelfth century, fresco.
Civate, Italy. Photography by Esmé Thompson.

more and more and more. In the first room it was a very condensed space with narrow pathways. Gradually the pathways opened up, so that the final space, winter, was these lit columns of hanging screens.

For maybe ten years I did these installations, and what I came to after I had explored that idea extensively was that I missed working in painting. While I had to have a plan and execute it, there wasn't this kind of reworking and changing in the process that comes with making a painting. This is part of what painting is about, and it is wonderful.

Then I did a body of work that was shaped canvases, multiple-part canvases. I was aware of Sean Scully and Elizabeth Murray and artists like that, and I was thinking about how the parts could be separate but a whole, and how you could move through the space of the painting, how space and even a sense of time changed because of the different rectangles. I did that body of work and then one day I was out in Claremont, New Hampshire, in a thrift store, and I saw this pile of things that looked like turtle shells or something. I didn't know what they were. They were all weathered, kind of funky metal, and I asked the guy about them. They were the tops of maple syrup buckets. I had always really loved the way those buckets look on the trees—it's so sad that they've replaced them with plastic tubes now. So I started ordering these tops and doing modular pieces. Instead of a surrounding space, it was a space in which I felt I could create dynamic movement by repetition. My interest in pattern started in that first piece, *Tops*, where I was working with iconography of "covering" derived from the bark of a tree, the covering of a shell, or the covering of a gravestone [fig. 3.3]. The first one was black and white and had collage—it was more built up—and then I made a piece called *Synecdoche* that was all about the idea of the skin, working with a palette of all reds and pinks. With these modular pieces I've tried to create a structure, not just with the relationship of the pattern to the individual parts, but to the outside shape of the entire piece—the way the modular units are displayed on the wall. That's led to a whole body of work.

BK: What do you think about symmetry?

ET: The metal pieces have been very symmetrical, because there's so much going on in them that I felt like they needed something schematic to create a balance. *Blue Divide*, which the Hood Museum of Art owns, and *Djellaba*, a new one, are very much based on symmetry, not just of outside shape but also of a contrasting and complementary color organization and mirrored patterns. I feel like they needed that kind of simplicity, so that I could work with all this interplay of pattern and drawing.

BK: And the convex nature of the image?

ET: The modular shape of the bucket cover is such a weird shape. It's got this kind of bent edge. It's not a perfect rectangle. Because it was somewhat sculptural, I felt I could decorate it with pattern that was flatter. I think about the edge and how the interior shapes relate to the edge, and you really have to consider the edge when you decorate it as you come up to that lip. The greatest decorated objects are really those kinds of spaces, decorated relative to that edge. I feel like I have a lot to learn, but I've been told, "You should make these volumes and you should think about that." I just think, "No, I can't! It's too much!" It starts to be sculpture, and I never have felt that my work is sculpture. I'm not that kind of a maker. That would require another lifetime, I think.

BK: Not all of your work has pieces in series with multiple parts. But the idea of seriality, of repetition, seems really important. You use seriality within the pieces of an individual work, and then you also make works in series. They're like species.

ET: I think the idea of seriality and grids comes out of the minimalist aesthetic. It also comes out of quilt making, and weaving, and even technology.

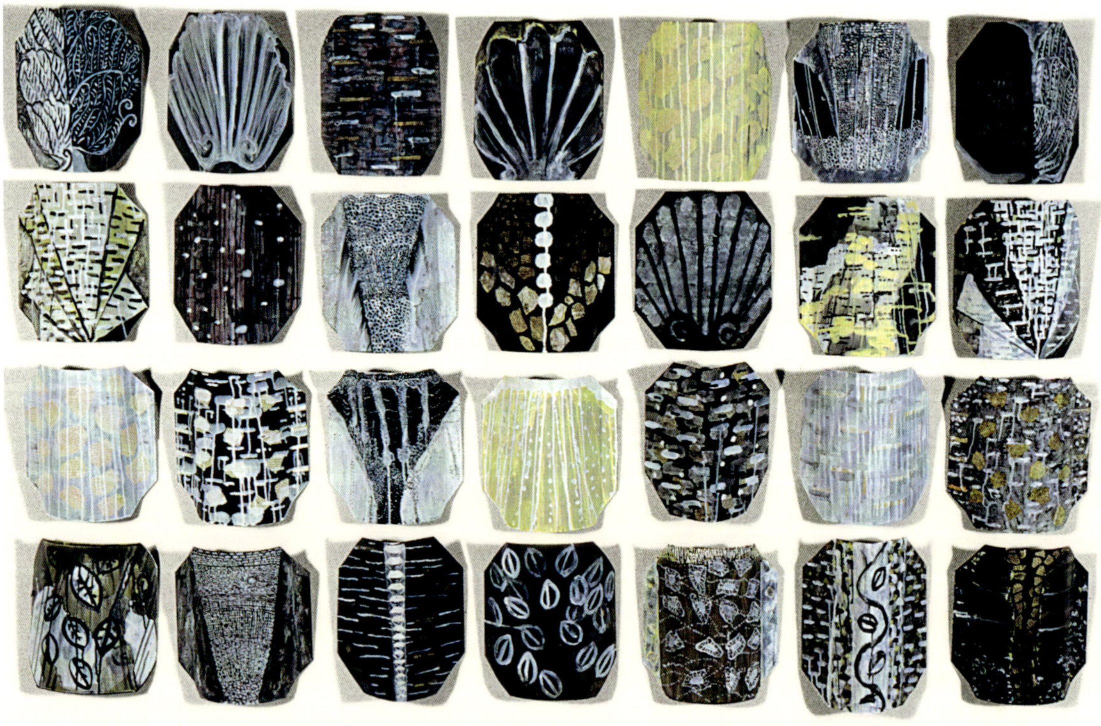

3.3. *Tops*, 1999, twenty-eight-piece installation, acrylic on metal. Photography by Esmé Thompson.

BK: I also think of repetition as repeated form done in multiples of variable numbers. Then, of course, there's the surface of your work and its use of repetition and variation.

ET: I know that I think about how certain types of pattern appear and reappear, and where they do.

BK: Well, maybe that leads directly to a discussion of your process, the stages of your work. Do you start with drawing or collage?

ET: A lot of times, I'll start with a collage. The collage allows me to put together elements that are of macrocosm and microcosm. A particular piece of collage may refer to architecture—to ornamental forms found in architecture. Another may be taken from a reference to a microscopic form. Or a piece of text. And they will be "woven" together.

BK: When you make a collage, are you cutting things out from published materials that you see? Describe the process of how you make them.

ET: I find these patterns that I just love. It's what really got me into using text for its visual quality in combination with references to the cellular, either a photograph or a drawing of cellular parts. Those could be juxtaposed in unexpected associations. The collage allowed that to happen. I've been really influenced from the very beginning by analytic cubism. I love those little fragments and how they can get all put together and become like drawing marks and shifting planes.

BK: When you make the collage and it has these designs on each individual cut-out shape, do you then change them when you make the paintings on canvas?

ET: It's just kind of a rough layout of what I want to do. For example, for the collage for *Djellaba,* I wanted a yellow diagonal movement down to the center. The left side's dominantly green and the right side's dominantly red. Of course, those colors get into the others; they mix, but in much smaller proportions, and then there are two center bands [fig. 3.4]. In that area of the installation the metal piece itself is not a curve, it's bent, and at those points I reverse the color structure. So on the red side, that side will be green, and vice versa. It's a very simple idea, but it allows me to really play with the pattern, because it's got that simple structure. I think that the simplest kind of color organization actually makes some of the greatest paintings, which is why I love Vuillard, because he worked so much with a warm and cool, a blue and an orange, complementary colors, and then he bases everything else on that, playing with that.

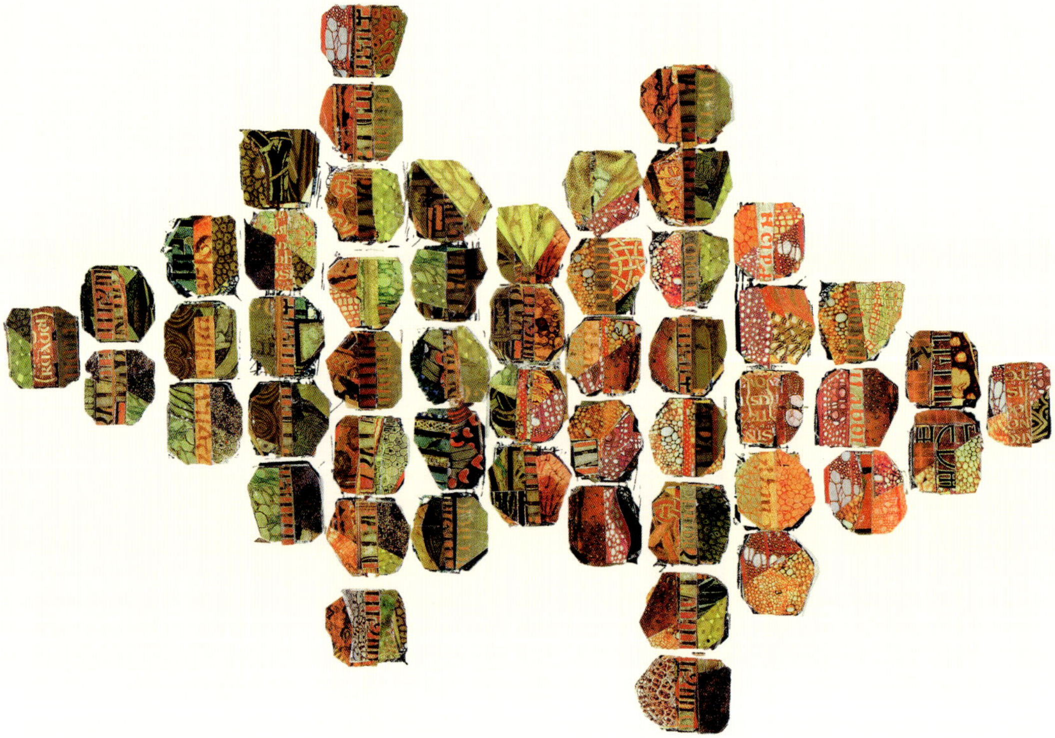

3.4. Study for *Djellaba,* 2010, collage.

BK: It's hard not to imagine that Matisse is important here.

ET: Well, Matisse *is* important. When I was thinking about *Djellaba,* I had in mind the shape of those robes for the Vence Chapel [the Chapel of the Rosary of the Dominican Nuns of Vence, France]; I was thinking about Berber woolen robes and realized, "Oh my God, it's just like the shape from the priest's robe for the Vence Chapel," but I have to be honest and say that I don't think I'm smart enough to understand everything that Matisse does. I feel in some ways like Vuillard is easier for me to understand. Matisse is so amazing in terms of the way he can pare things down and make his decisions. Of course I love him.

And place is important too. I went to Italy in 1978, and then in, I think, 1993, I applied to the Rockefeller Foundation to do a response to that chapel in Civate right near the Bellagio. And I got there and I was just so happy. I had this little studio down by the water. I'd walk down the hill through the olive orchard and do these paintings. I just fell in love with Italy. So then I went back again to a place called the Bogliasco Foundation near Genoa, and I've gone back there three times. It's where I've gotten some of my best work done. I feel inspired and at home.

The first time I went to Bogliasco, I met Marjorie Woods, and she said, "You've got to see the Archivio de Stato in Sienna. It has all these painted wooden book covers, and they're just like your work!" And so I went and I was very lucky to get in to see them. They were the treasury records for the city of Sienna, and they were narrative and very patterned [see fig. 1.4]. Sometimes they had these leather hinges with metal grommets on them. They were about the same proportions as my metal pieces and a similar palette. They're just phenomenal.

BK: Your work is fascinating to me because you embrace biology, nature, landscape, books, text, English—there's a tremendous sense of fascination with the decorative, and I wanted to address that particularly, because Matisse really was the first to try, in his later years, to make the decorative acceptable, as opposed to pejorative. And then many other artists have engaged in that. I know you say you don't need to make a political statement and you don't want to bring anger into the studio, but your work really is incredibly life enhancing; I mean, it's not in any way depressing.

ET: That's what I hope for. An artist that I admire is Philip Taafe. I think he's thinking that you can choose to be celebratory, and to hope that the boundaries can be erased between "high" and "low" art. At least to celebrate the kinds of things that people have made, and the fact that the people who have carried culture forward have been the poor people a lot of the time. When I was in Morocco, I worked in the Fez Pottery Cooperative. Unassuming people are decorating these incredible dishes, and they're learning by memorizing the pattern. They're not allowed to look at anything else. They look at the pattern; they incorporate it; and that's what they told us, because we were painting too. "Do not look over there at the original design. Look at it first, remember it, and paint it." And that's what they do, and they carry that forward. And maybe it's going to get lost, because all of these crafts are being taken over by the West.

BK: In terms of contemporary culture, and this is related to the capacity of digital animation, do you work with computers?

ET: I've used digital media. I've taken a photograph of a painting or collage and then played around with it digitally to get a color idea. These programs are great tools, but I really love things that have the human, handmade touch. Even though with my work, sometimes the skin is very thin, I still touch every little piece of it. It's like mosaic tile in Morocco. Every single tile has had four different people touch it. They've made the tile, they've cut the tile, they've glazed the tile, and then they've beveled the tile. So when you see these *zellij* walls, you realize the human touch. It's not machine made. It's just totally compulsive, totally crazy, but every single thing is made by an individual. When I was at the Tyrone Guthrie Foundation in Ireland, I was up in my studio, bent over, looking at the lace, and doing a painting from their lace collection [see fig. 2.4]. I thought I was just like those nuns or priests painting illuminated manuscripts, and I felt like I was making some kind of connection there.

BK: The detail in your work requires great perseverance. Does that have a meditative quality for you?

ET: Yes. I'm here day after day. The ritual of the process is important to me. Also, these things aren't flying off the wall, so I can spend as much time as I want on them. I love it. I get lost in it. It's that idea of being inside the painting. These things, like the color—maybe four different washes of color, drawn into, painted into, and sometimes I sand them and repaint. Why not spend your life doing that?

BK: Would you talk about the nature of your surfaces?

ET: I've gone through a lot of phases in my work. I had a whole series of pieces that were based on the iconography of *The Annunciation* [see fig. 1.1]. They were about transformation, about movement from one space into another space. Those paintings were much more built up. There's a piece called *Boomerang* that was an installation made of triangles that moved around the space of two gallery walls at the Fitchburg Museum [fig. 3.5]. They were pairs of triangles, and they went through the range of the whole color wheel, so they started with a blue, maybe, and then ended up at the other end of the spectrum. Those

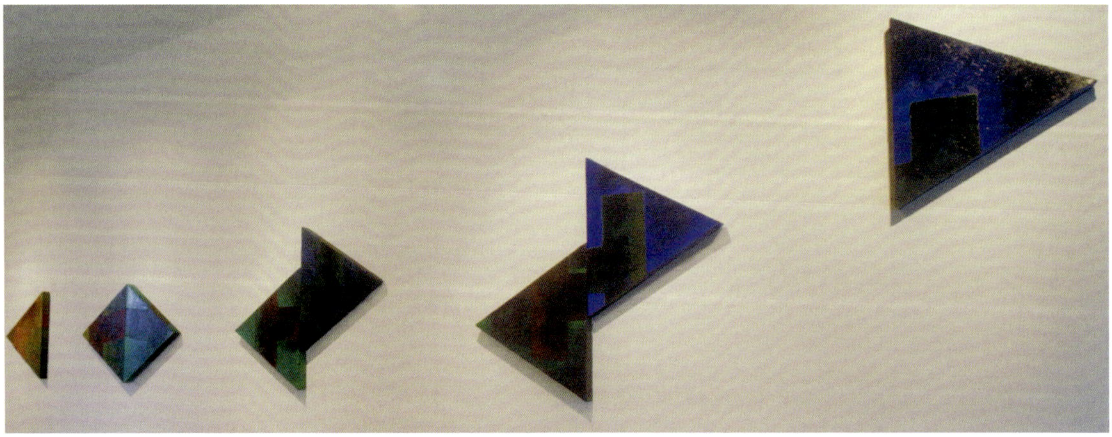

3.5. *Boomerang*, 1992, installation at Fitchburg Art Museum, Fitchburg, Mass. Photography by Esmé Thompson.

were really thickly painted and very glossy. But for the last several years, I've been painting very thinly. I feel like these paintings are still drawings in a way. Right now they're starting to get a little more built up because I'm putting oil back into them. I found I could get the luminosity I wanted with the transparency, which I grew to love from working on the metal. You can't put paint on too thick on these things, or you lose that kind of glow. So I started liking that, and when I went back to board and canvas, I was working thinner again, and I could get that kind of layered color, but I don't really feel like I think one way of working's better than the other, it's just where I am right now.

BK: The materiality is important, isn't it, with you?

ET: Yes, but if there's one thing I've learned after going through an abstract expressionist phase at the very beginning of my artistic career, it's that thick painting is no better than thin painting. When I was at Yale, there was a feeling that you had to be this kind of macho painter and really lay on the paint, and a lot of us bought into that to be part of the group. But you don't have to do that anymore. You can do any kind of work you want to do these days.

BK: Do you know a book by Joseph Masheck called *The Carpet Paradigm*? His theory is that abstraction, and particularly the pursuit of flatness, came out of the nineteenth-century absorption with carpets, and particularly the Arabesque version of carpets. For some people, it might be a bit of a stretch, but it actually is incredibly informative regarding so much twentieth-century art. The reason I asked is that you mentioned Morocco. The carpet is flat but it can invite you, either on the wall or on the floor, to enter into it. You're initially entering into it by standing on it, of course, if it's on the floor. But that idea of space and illusion is very important to your work. So maybe we might talk about that again, the extent to which your work is illusionistic and the extent to which your work provides this, it seems to me, extraordinary sense of depth, and yet you have this preoccupation with skin and flesh and surface.

ET: Yes, it's interesting. Space has always been an important issue in my work. But eventually I realized I could make the feeling of spatial movement across the picture plane by making these patterned visual connections, and that became much more important to me. I got really interested in how space was organized in medieval painting, where it's a hierarchical space about who the narrative's about and what's more important than what else, so you could put a great big figure next to a tiny little figure, and they could be side by side. You get to that in Vuillard too, he's got these paintings with a great big figure going top to bottom of the canvas, and right next to it is a tiny little figure. And everybody says that's about his interest in photography, but I think he also knows about early Renaissance and earlier systems of perspective.

BK: What is it about Vuillard that fascinates you, that makes you really resonate with him?

ET: I think about that a lot, because if you look at my paintings, I'm not really working with his color. I feel like it kind of goes back to your question about the symmetrical quality. He gives me a framework to hang the painting on. *Madame Vuillard Reading the Newspaper* is a painting of his in the Phillips collection—I've worked from it over and over again, because I love the contradictions and tensions of space and pattern that he sets up, and the idea of this vibrating, scintillating color. Then I take off in my own direction and it just keeps transforming.

BK: You have a very distinctive style. I mean, if part of the artistic career is to find your voice, there's absolutely no doubt that you have.

ET: Elizabeth Murray said, "It's taken me my whole life working toward my style, and I hope at the end of my life, I'm finding my style."

BK: You have, it seems, a very distinctive range. There's a high key, I would say, a high pitch to your color. But with the sense of symmetry is also harmony. They're very harmonious. The danger would be, if you thought musically, that it might be dissonant, and yet it's all matched with this sense of repetition and harmony, and it's very beautiful. It makes me wonder about your relationship to gardens and to flowers, and I also find a reptilian aspect to some of your work.

ET: Skin, or the patterns found on something you find in the garden [fig. 3.6]. That often comes from my interpretation of a cellular drawing. As far as being "beautiful," what I want for my work is that it be a celebration of life.

BK: And physically, when you began a painting, where did you start?

ET: With everything I do, I work all over.

BK: This interest that you have in medieval painting, medieval illumination—there's religious, sort of hieratic imagery, and then there's secular imagery, like the woman reading. There's also something about the Middle Ages that's generally attractive to you.

ET: It started with my interest in art that was made before the invention of perspective. The spaces are just so seductive to me. They're so abstract; they're so modern, in a way. But also I've gotten really involved in this series of paintings that are women's side views of women. I put up this little tile I bought in Italy one time, and it was the first one that made me think, "Oh, a side view of a woman [see fig. 2.7]." It's like a shape I can use and have a feeling of a figure in a painting in a different way, and so it just set off this whole body of work.

BK: You mentioned vestments. Your works would be very beautiful robes.

ET: It's just so interesting, the margin between decorating and evoking decoration. Philip Taafe does not consider that his work is decorative, but I'm not as concerned about that definition.

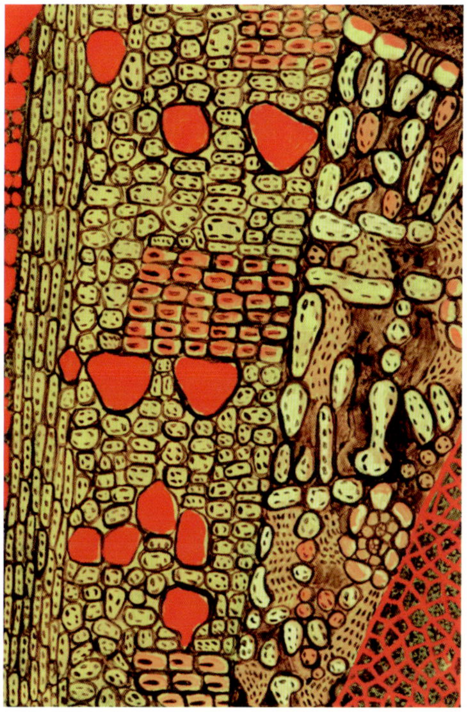

3.6. Detail of *Djellaba*, 2010, acrylic on metal.

BK: So how would you feel if your work was described as decorative?

ET: I think that would be a compliment. After what I've seen and what I know, for example, there are women working in caves making carpets that are so much greater than that collage, and they're weaving holding the fiber with their toes. I don't want to think that painting is better than some of these great objects of decoration, and I wish I knew how to make some of these things.

BK: I want to read something to you—Arthur Danto describes the pattern and decoration movement and the way it sought to, in his words, "obliterate the distinction between art and decoration." He thought it was "an early step into globalist esthetics."

ET: It began the multicultural movement in the 1970s, which became the hip, postmodern thing to do. But even earlier, they had a show at the Whitney with quilts displayed alongside the work of artists like Noland and other color field painters, and it's like they were elevating the quilts. But quilt makers were working with the same colors and forms long before these artists. Or to think about how stitching is like drawing. And the modesty of it, too. Somehow that means something to me; that these artisans don't think the objects they make are fantastic, they just make them because they think they're important to have in people's lives. To me, I find that so elevating, so uplifting. It's why I want to travel and learn.

BK: How has your role as a professor interacted with your role as a practitioner? Has one fed the other?

ET: In some ways, I keep them kind of separate. I really love teaching drawing. It's just an amazing thing to get students to learn how to see. Because people don't look, and it's amazing what a struggle it is to get them to look, and when they do, all of a sudden, it's really like a light bulb goes on. Sometimes it goes around the class, when all of a sudden they can see the things they're looking at. And then to realize how they can invent and think through this kind of physical activity, the visual and the physical. It's a really great gift to give somebody and that gift just energizes you.

And then I started teaching collage a couple of years ago. I have found that collage is another way to draw, another way to think about things, and it connects you with the physical possibilities of something. I personally think that most postmodernist art is a kind of collage. It's perfect for students. And so I've enjoyed thinking about how you can draw with collage, or paint with collage, or all those things—how those things can interconnect.

BK: How would you describe what you've sought to do as a professor?

ET: At Dartmouth I've worked as a part of a wonderful faculty that's making a department that's really unique in undergraduate arts education. To help students understand what this activity of studio research is. You're researching the world you live in and the culture you live in, but you're also researching yourself, your personal intellectual, emotional, spiritual ideas. Trying to tap into that. I guess that comes out in an unconscious way, at least in my work. I feel that I can't help but have it come out. But for me it's always about the discipline. I remember John Walker used to say, "If you don't get in the studio for five days, you're in trouble." And I understand that. I have to be in here making all the time. I have to keep that connection going. Sometimes it's a hard thing to convince students of that.

BK: You brought up the word discipline. What are the values that have caused you to be able to persist?

ET: It isn't hard for me. There's nothing else I want to do, really. Sometimes I think, "What would I do if I didn't go into the studio?" Ever since that first experience at Yale Norfolk, where I felt what it was like to just be non-stop in the studio, it was all I ever wanted to do. I think to have a life where you can do what I do, you're really fortunate, you know?

BK: It seems that whatever travails in life you might have had, your work seems to operate on a plane that doesn't reflect periods of great turmoil or angst.

ET: I do think that when you're going through a trauma, your work shows it, whether you think so or not. I agree with what you say in the sense that I have always been able to put aside things that are difficult. I've had a lot of situations where, if I had immersed myself in them, I wouldn't have been able to do my work, so I just haven't let myself do that.

BK: To return to something you said at the beginning, about how we were looking at three decades here, and for two of them you wanted to be in New York, and then in the third you maybe accepted that you were going to be in the Upper Valley. How have you reconciled that? There's a busyness in your work that sort of feels at once very city-like and yet garden-like too. The garden's just full of vibrancy and possibility.

ET: Well, I make sure that I get my work out in the world. Otherwise you're just making it to stick in a cabinet, and I feel art should be a form of communication. For example, for the installation work it is really important to find specific sites. And I have very good friends that I try to see, and I try to get to New York to see good shows. When I go down to New York, I see that it's just so hard for artists to live there now. So I don't feel the necessity to move to New York anymore. I just feel like, because I haven't been there, I've had more time to get my work done. I have plenty of friends that are still struggling in New York.

BK: Tell me about your titles. You don't use *Untitled*, for example.

ET: The titles come at the very end and often reflect something I feel about the work, or another take on the piece. For the whole series called *Tipsy*, I just thought these looked like that idea, but also the heads are tipping in all different directions [fig. 3.7]. All the ones that come from rhetoric, they started out because I was at the Liguria Study Center in Bogliasco, Italy, and Ruth Katz, a Professor of Musicology from Hebrew University in Israel, came in and said, "Oh, a good title for this painting would be *Metonymy*, the parts represented by the whole, and I just said, "Okay."

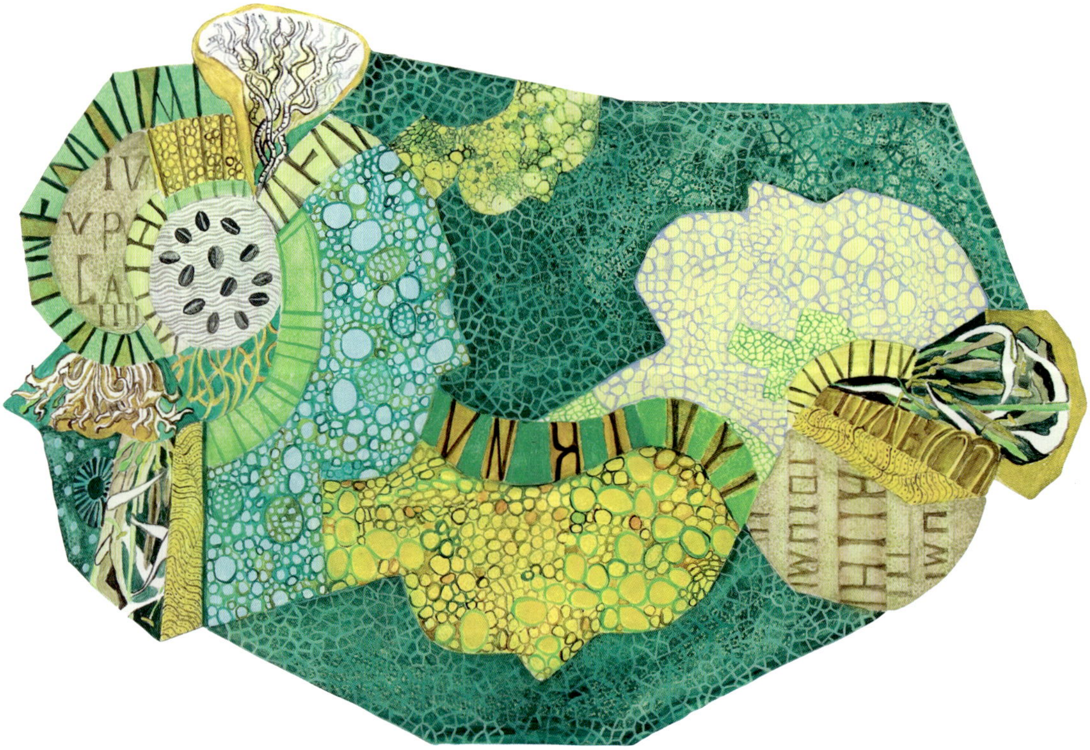

3.7. *Tipsy III*, 2008, acrylic on board. Photography by Hathorne/Olson.

BK: What about your work's relationships to mosaic and stained glass?

ET: I saw the Byzantine show at the Met quite a few years ago. I actually saw it with Marjorie Woods, and she could read the text in the paintings. There were these paintings made of tiny little pieces of tile or mosaic, and they went right around the contour of a face. You think of those icon paintings as being so flat, but they weren't flat. These were so volumetric and subtle. I really loved them. It's fun to think that every little mark you make makes a movement. When there are so many, sometimes you don't notice at first.

BK: In terms of your working day, do you begin at a particular time and leave at a particular time?

ET: I try to come in and work in the morning. I don't work at night. I work best if I can have at least four or five hours in a row—a block of time. I have friends that work day and night, but I just don't do that anymore. Sometimes it works well for me to have two or three things that I'm working on.

BK: The earlier work, the installations made for site-specific places, were they hard to sell?

ET: Those installations were not meant to be permanent. Works like *Marine Corridors* [fig. 3.8] were site specific and temporary. That is the liberation of being in an academic community, the ideal of an academic community: the freedom that you have to pursue your ideas without having to worry about financial consequences. It's given me freedom to do things that don't sell. Of course, I would love to be in a situation where people wanted to own my work and put it up on their walls, but I don't feel like that's the reason I do the work.

BK: There's a tremendous sense of confidence in your work.

ET: Maybe it's just naïveté. I remember at Yale Norfolk, Louis Finkelstein gave us this assignment to paint with a palette of colors, a triad, and to paint like a Seurat pointillist painting. So we all set up in a landscape and we're painting away, and he came around after half an hour, and he said to me, "You're doing it all wrong! That's not what I said to do . . . But that's a good painting, so just never mind."

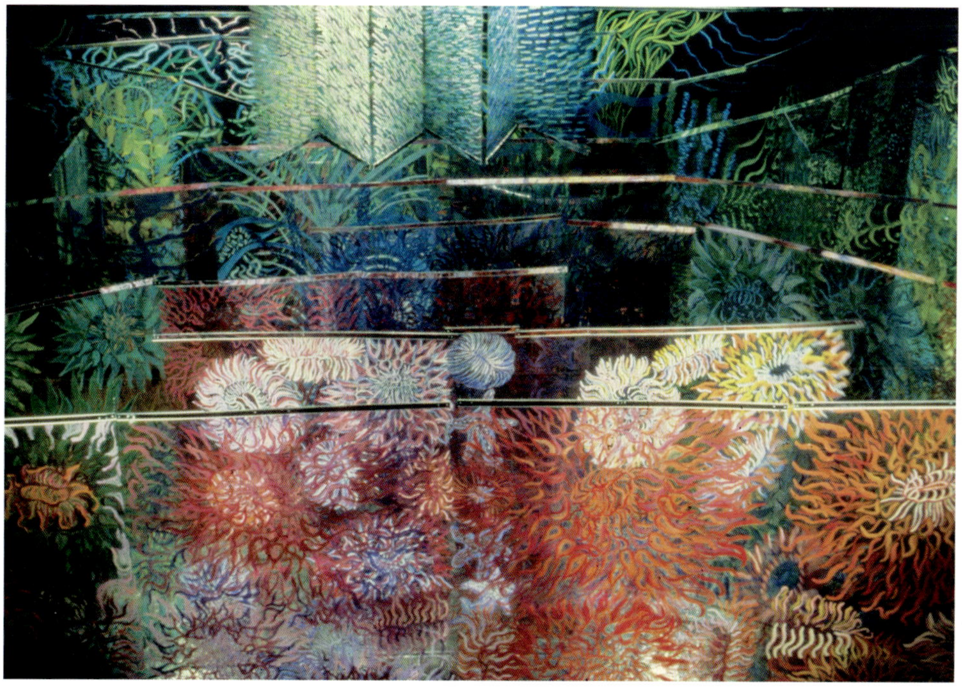

3.8. *Marine Corridors*, 1983, installation at Real Art Ways, Hartford, Conn. Photography by Esmé Thompson.

Esmé Thompson: Selected Record

Pamela E. Thompson Born La Jolla, CA, 1946 Resides Lebanon, NH

SOLO EXHIBITIONS

2011 *Esmé Thompson: Alchemy of Design*, Hood Museum of Art, Dartmouth College, Hanover, NH, April–June

2010 Strauss Gallery, Dartmouth College, Hanover, NH, March

2008 Bowery Gallery, NYC, December

2007 Les Yeux du Monde, Charlottesville, VA, September

2006 Mercer Gallery, NYC

2005 New England College, Henniker, NH, September

2004 Humanities Fine Arts Gallery, University of Minnesota, Morris, October; 55 Mercer Gallery, NYC

1999 55 Mercer Gallery, NYC

1997 The Painting Center, NYC; Widener Gallery, Trinity College, Hartford, CT

1996 Curfman Gallery, Colorado State University, Fort Collins, CO

1995 Carney Gallery, Fine Arts Center, St. Regis College, Weston, MA

1993 Hobart and William Smith College, Geneva, NY; Kimball Bourgault Gallery, Boston

1992 Second Street Gallery, Charlottesville, VA; Tyler Gallery, Marlboro College, Marlboro, VT; *Boomerang*, Fitchburg Museum, Fitchburg, MA, curator: Linda Poras

1990 Jaffe-Friede Gallery, Dartmouth College, Hanover, NH; Chapel Art Center, Saint Anselm College, Manchester, NH

1989 *The Jericho Installation*, Rosenburg Gallery, Goucher College, Baltimore, funded by a grant from the Maryland State Arts Council and the National Endowment for the Arts

1987 *Arcade*, Florence Wilcox Gallery, Swarthmore College, Swarthmore, PA; *Phoenix* Installation, Cambridge Multicultural Arts Center, Cambridge, MA

1986 *Phoenix* Installation, Duxbury Art Museum, Duxbury, MA; *Varanasi Reverse* (installation), Barrows Rotunda, Hopkins Center for the Performing Arts, Dartmouth College, Hanover, NH

1984 *Cycles* (installation), Lamont Gallery, Frederick Mayer Art Center, Phillips Exeter Academy, Exeter, NH; *Blooms* (installation), Sarah Doyle Gallery, Brown University, Providence, RI

1983 Installation, Thorne-Sagendorph Gallery, Keene State College, Keene, NH; installation, Warner Bentley Theatre, Hopkins Center for the Performing Arts, Dartmouth College, Hanover, NH; *Marine Corridors* (installation), Real Art Ways, Hartford, CT

1982 *Corridors* (installation), Langton Arts, San Francisco; Salena Gallery, Long Island University, Brooklyn, NY

GROUP EXHIBITIONS

2009 New acquisitions, Hood Museum of Art, Dartmouth College, Hanover, NH, September

2008 Two-person show, Helen Day Art Center, Stowe, VT, June

2007 Brattleboro Museum, Brattleboro, VT, December; four-person show, List Gallery, Swarthmore College, Swarthmore, PA, November; Studio Art Faculty Exhibition, Jaffe-Friede Gallery, Dartmouth College, Hanover, NH, November

2006 Spheris Gallery, Hanover, NH; *Networks and Intersections*, New Newton Art Center, Newton, MA

2005 The Art Gallery, Paul Creative Arts Center, University of New Hampshire, Durham, NH, November; Cambridge Art Association National Prize Show, Cambridge, MA, May, juror: Joseph Thompson, Director MassMOCA; Faculty Art Exhibition, Jaffe-Friede and Strauss Galleries, Dartmouth College, Hanover, NH, April; *Works on Paper*, Gross McCleaf Gallery, Philadelphia, March

2004 Three-person show, Washington Art Association, Washington Depot, CT; three-person show, Grimshaw Gudewicz Art Gallery, Bristol, MA

2003 Tenth Annual Juried Show, Essex Art Center, Lawrence, MA, juror: Jock Reynolds, Director, Yale University Art Gallery

2002 Two-person show, Brenda Garand and Esmé Thompson, 55 Mercer Gallery, NYC

2001 Four-person show, Charles Burwell, Andrew Forge, Esmé Thompson, Roger Tibbetts, 55 Mercer Gallery, NYC, May; two-person show, Edward Hopper Art Center, Nyack, NY

2000 Three-person show, Colby Sawyer College, New London, NH, September; two-person show, AVA Gallery, Lebanon, NH; Faculty Art Exhibition, Jaffe-Friede and Strauss Galleries, Dartmouth College, Hanover, NH; *Generations II*, A.I.R. Gallery, NYC; E. J. Vaughn Associates, NYC

1999 *Convergence: Works on Paper*, New England College, Henniker, NH

1998 Two-person show, Lenore Gray Gallery, Providence, RI

1997 Takara Gallery, Houston, TX; Faculty Art Exhibition, Jaffe-Friede and Strauss Galleries, Dartmouth College, Hanover, NH; *Architicture into Art*, three-person show, Samuel Chen Gallery, Central Connecticut State University, New Britain, CT

1996 *Geometric Perspective: Loosely Speaking*, Pearl Conard Gallery, Ohio State University, Mansfield, OH; *Drawing: A Way of Thinking*, Chautauqua School of Art, Chautauqua, NY

1995 *Imagining Angels*, Howard Yezerski Gallery, Boston; Provincetown Art Association and Museum, Provinceton, MA; three-person show, Chaffee Art Center, Rutland, VT; Invitational Group Show, Bowery Gallery, NYC

1994 Brenda Taylor Gallery, Boston

1993 Faculty Art Exhibition, Jaffe-Friede and Strauss Galleries, Dartmouth College, Hanover, NH; Newton Arts Center, Newtonville, MA

1991 *Decade of Excellence Exhibit*, Library Arts Center, Newport, NH; *Abstract Art*, Warwick Museum, Warwick, RI, curator: Len Long, RISD

1990 Berkshire Art Association Works on Paper, The Berkshire Museum, Pittsfield, MA, juror: Charlotta Kotik, Curator of Contemporary Art, Brooklyn Museum

1989 *Nancy Graves Chooses Works on Paper*, Artspace, New Haven, CT, juror: Nancy Graves; Phillips Brickman Gallery, Brookline, MA; *Layerings*, two-person show, Newton Arts Center, Newtonville, MA, curator: Helen Shlien; Ninth Annual Faber Birren Color Award Show, Stamford Art Association, Stamford, CT, juror: Charlotta Kotik, Curator of Contemporary Art, Brooklyn Museum; *Vermont Selections*, Helen Day Art Center, Stowe, VT

1988 Invitational Group Show, Bowery Gallery, NYC

1987 *Transparency/Translucency*, Aljira Arts, Newark, NJ; *Stone Forest*, Dartmouth College, Hanover, NH

1985 Drawings and Paintings, Michael Rockefeller Art Center, State University College at Fredonia, Fredonia, NY; Faculty Exhibition, Chautauqua Art Association Gallery, Chautauqua Institution, Chautauqua, NY

1982 *Spiral Poppy* (installation), Barrows Rotunda, Hopkins Center for the Performing Arts, Dartmouth College, Hanover, NH; *Weftworks*, Atrium Gallery, Claremont Opera House, Claremont, NH

SELECTED EXHIBITIONS PRE-1980

1978 Yale University Drawing Show, University of Melbourne, Australia

1975 Mid-Mississippi Annual, Municipal Art Gallery, Davenport, IA; 27th Annual Art Exhibition, Spokane Museum of Art, Spokane, WA

EXHIBITION REVIEWS

Boston Globe, Cate McQuaid, February 2, 2006

Art New England, Dustin Knight, vol. 27, no. 2, 2006

Hartford Courant, Jude Schwendenwien, April 5, 1997

Hartford Advocate, Patricia Rosoff, March 27, 1997

Art New England, Margot Clark, December/January 1989/1990

Boston Sunday Herald, Nancy Stapen, November 19, 1989

Boston Globe, Christine Temin, November 23, 1989

Maryland Live, *The Baltimore Sun*, John Dorsey, March 17, 1989

Art New England, Jessica Potter, October 1983

Boston Sunday Globe, Robert Taylor, September 30, 1984

Hartford Courant, Bernard Hanson, July 24, 1983

San Francisco Chronicle, Suzaan Boettger, June 22, 1982

CATALOGUES

"Icons," essay by Rosemary Noon, Carney Gallery, Regis College, Weston, MA, October 1995

"Installation Art," essay by Linda Poras, Fitchburg Art Museum, Fitchburg, MA, February 1992

Jaffe-Friede exhibition; essays by Jim Cuno, Director, Hood Museum of Art, and Susan Mareneck, artist; Dartmouth College, Hanover, NH, November 1990

"The Jericho Installation," essay by Helen Glazer, Rosenberg Gallery, Goucher College, Baltimore, March 1989

"Painted Installations," essay by Suzanne Foley, Langton Arts, San Francisco, 1983

COLLECTIONS

Hood Museum of Art, Dartmouth College, Hanover, NH

Anderson Consulting, Washington, DC

American Council on Education, Washington, DC

Diane Johnson, The Providence Group, Providence, RI

Merion Investors LLC, Westfield, NJ

Babson College, Wellesley, MA

Sally and Chris Lutz, Woodstock, VT

Goodwin, Proctor and Hoar, Boston

Eleanor Schneider, Rutland, VT

Hotel Cosima, Tokyo

AWARDS

Senior Faculty Fellowship, Ritratti: An Exploration of Multiple-Plate Color Printmaking at Wingate Press, 2010–11

The John Sloan Dickey Center for International Understanding Research Grant: A Study of Ornament and Decoration in Zillij, Moroccan Ceramic Wall Relief, January 2010

Leslie Center for the Humanities, Faculty Travel and Research Grant, A Study of Ornament and Decoration in Zillij, Moroccan Ceramic Wall Relief, January 2010

Bogliasco Foundation Fellowship, Liguria, Italy, February–March 2008

Tyrone Guthrie Centre, Annaghmakerrig, County Monaghan, Ireland, Residency, fall 2004

Bogliasco Foundation Fellowship, Liguria, Italy, February–March 2003

Senior Faculty Fellowship, Dartmouth College, Hanover, NH, spring 2000

Bogliasco Foundation Fellowship, Liguria, Italy, spring 1999

Mellon Foundation Grant, Hood Museum of Art, Dartmouth College, spring 1998

Honorary Degree, Master of Arts, Dartmouth College, February 1993

Rockefeller Foundation Fellowship, Bellagio, Italy, winter 1993

Villa Montalvo Residency, Saratoga, CA, winter 1992

Senior Faculty Fellowship, Dartmouth College, Hanover, NH, fall 1991

Vermont State Council on the Arts Award, 1986

Kenneth Huntington Teaching Award, Dartmouth College, 1986

Ford Foundation Grant, 1985

Member, Copley Society of Boston, 1984–85

NH Commission on the Arts Grant, 1983

Faculty Fellowship, Dartmouth College, winter 1982–83

Yale University scholarships, 1977–78.

Ford Foundation special project grant, Yale University, 1978

Shickle Collingwood Award, Yale University, 1977

EDUCATION

Yale University, New Haven, CT, MFA (Painting), 1978

University of Iowa, Iowa City, MA (Painting), 1976

Yale Summer Session for Music and Art, Norfolk, CT, summer 1975

Studio School, Spokane, WA, 1973–75

Whitworth College, Spokane, WA, BA (English), 1968

TEACHING

Professor of Studio Art, Dartmouth College, 1979–present; Chair, 1994–97; Acting Chair, 1987–88; Acting Chair, summers, 1989–92

Visiting Instructor in Drawing, Chautauqua Institution, Art Center, summer 1996

Visiting Professor, Princeton University, fall 1989

Director, Art Center, Chautauqua Institution, summer 1985

Visiting Professor, RISD, fall 1984

Visiting Instructor, Royal College of Art, London, summer 1978

VISITING ARTIST

Visiting Critic, American University's Study Abroad Program, Corciano, Italy, December 2000

Visiting Critic, Trinity College, October 1997

Lecture, "Art into Architecture," Central Connecticut State University, April 1997

Visiting Artist/Slide Lecture, Colorado State University, October 1996

Visiting Artist, Carleton College, Northfield, MN, April 1995

Visiting Artist, Trinity College, Hartford, CT, March 1995

Lecture, Hobart and William Smith College, Geneva, NY, October 1993

Lecture, Trinity College, Hartford, CT, March 1993

Visiting Artist, RISD, Providence, RI, November 1992

Lecture, American University, Washington, DC, April 1992

Lecture, Dartmouth College, Hanover, NH, 1990

Lecture, "Layerings," Newton Art Center, Newtonville, MA, November 1989

Lecture, Goucher College, Baltimore, March 1989

Lecture, Montclair State College, Governor's Challenge Grant for Excellence, Upper Montclair, NJ, November 1988

Lecture, Dartmouth Institute, July 1988

Lecture, Swarthmore College, Swarthmore, PA, November 1987

Visiting Artist, Yale University, New Haven, CT, July 1987

Lecture, Dartmouth Institute, July 1987

Juror for AVA Gallery Summer Exhibition, Hanover, NH, 1987

Lecture, "Challenging the Painted Plane," Dartmouth Institute, March 1986

Juror for 22nd Annual Stratton Arts Festival, 1985

Juror for Ralph Bradley Art Show, Phillips Exeter Academy, 1985

Phillips Exeter Academy, September 1984

Lecture, RISD, Providence, RI, March 1984

Juror for "Regional Selections," Hopkins Center for the Performing Arts, Dartmouth College, 1982

GALLERY AFFILIATION

Bowery Gallery, NYC

Works in the Exhibition

All works are in the collection of the artist, unless otherwise indicated.

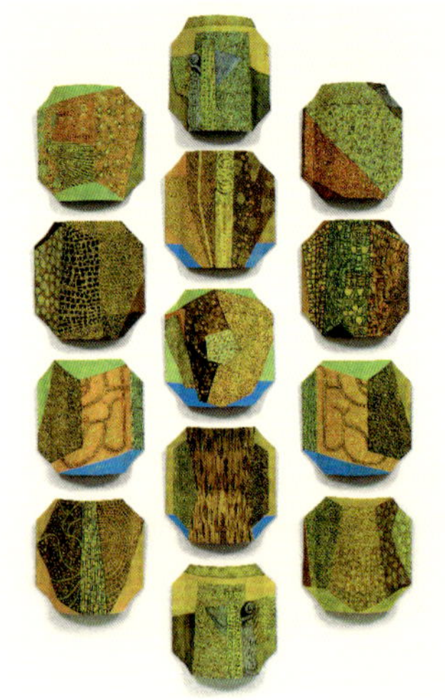

1. ***Beatus II,*** 2003
Thirteen-piece installation; acrylic on metal
69 x 42 x 3 inches

2. ***Liggia I,*** 2003
Acrylic on canvas
68 x 38 inches

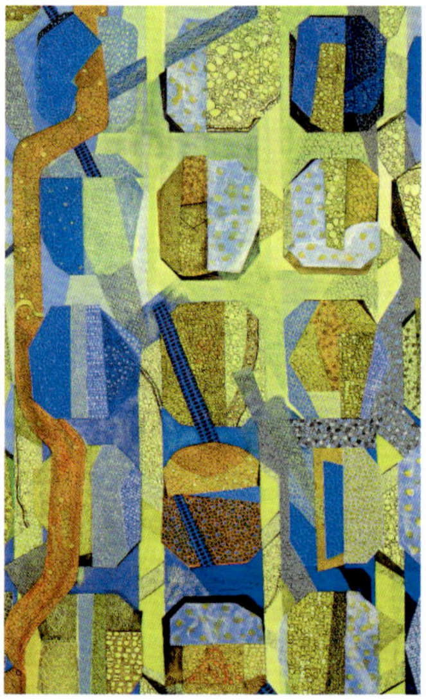

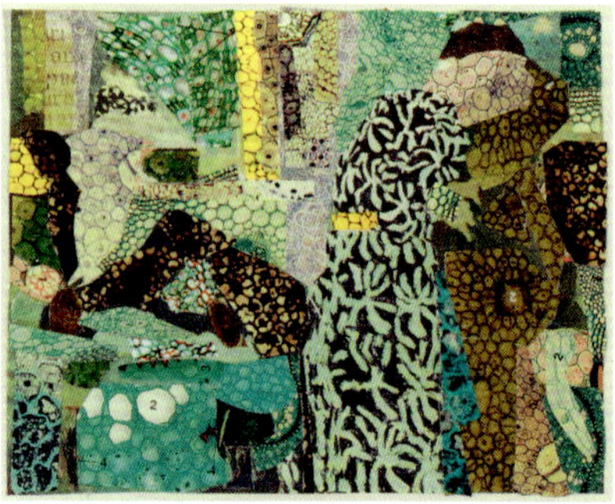

3. ***After Vuillard/Annaghmakerrig,*** 2004
Collage
5 x 6 inches

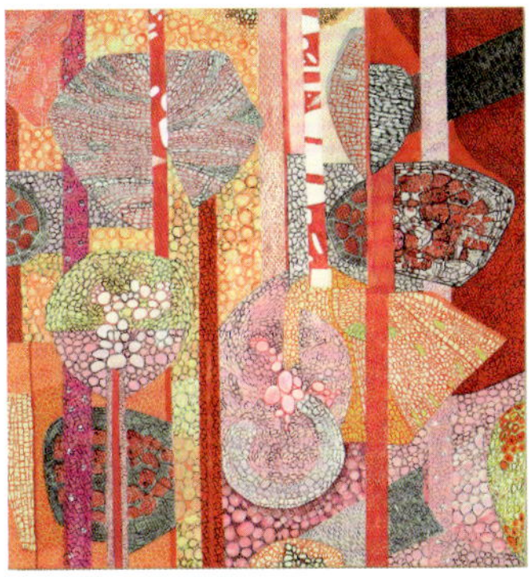

4. ***Ornamentum I,*** 2004
Acrylic on canvas
48 x 44 inches

5. ***Blue Divide,*** 2005
Forty-nine-piece installation;
acrylic on metal, 94 x 194 x 3 inches
Hood Museum of Art, Dartmouth College: Purchased through the William S. Rubin Fund: 2008.11

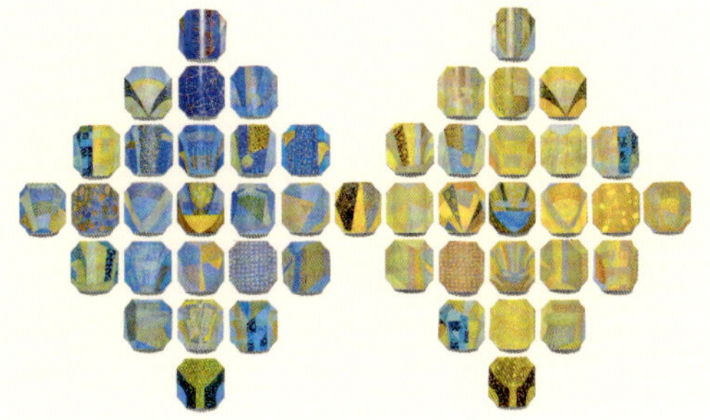

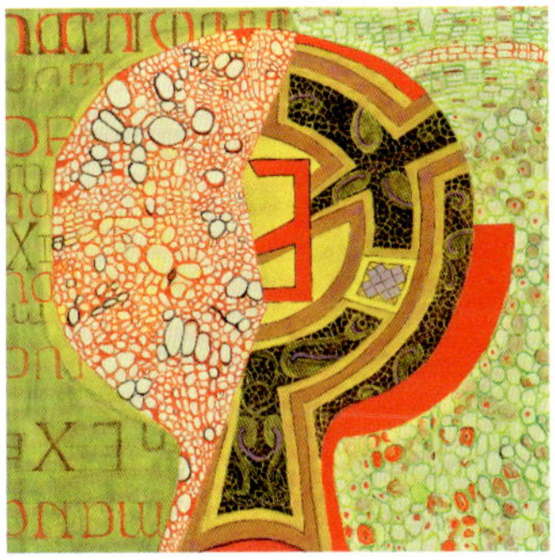

6. ***Credo,*** 2005
Acrylic on board
24 x 24 inches

7. ***Ornamentum IV,*** 2005
Acrylic on canvas
48 x 42 inches

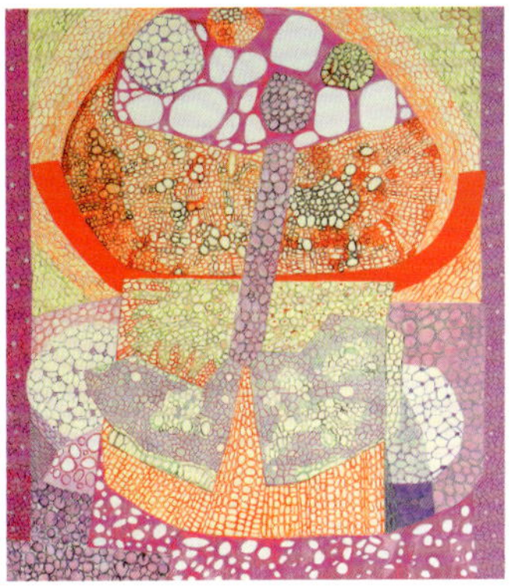

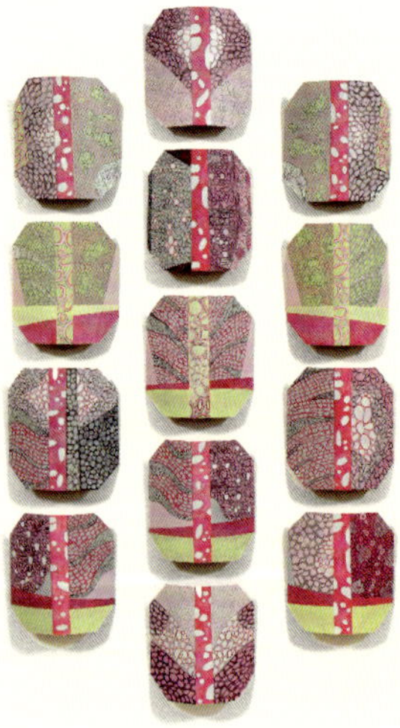

8. ***Ornamentum V,***
right side, 2005
Thirteen-piece installation;
acrylic on metal
72 x 42 x 3 inches

9. ***Lisant III,*** 2006
Acrylic on board
24 x 36 inches

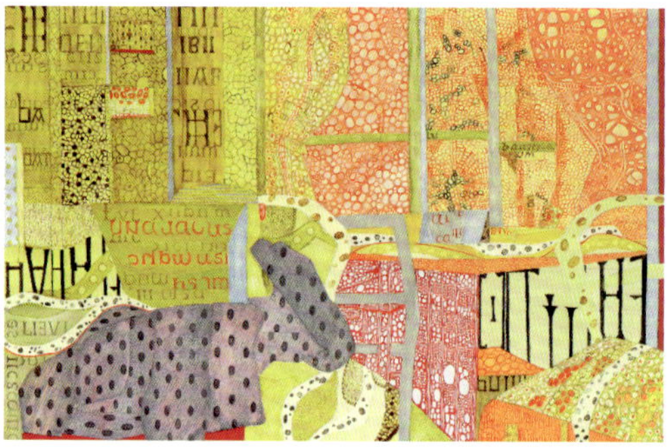

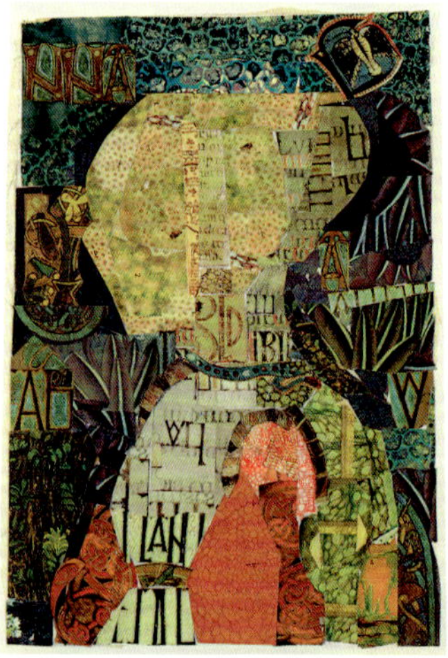

10. ***After Pisanello,*** 2007
Collage
11 x 8 inches

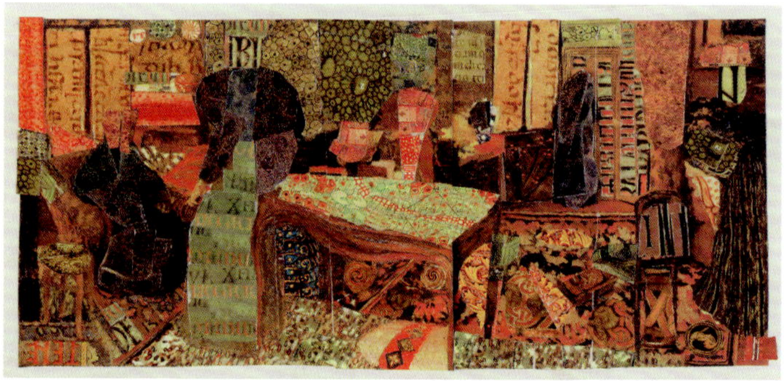

11. ***After Vuillard IV,*** 2007
Collage
6 x 14 inches

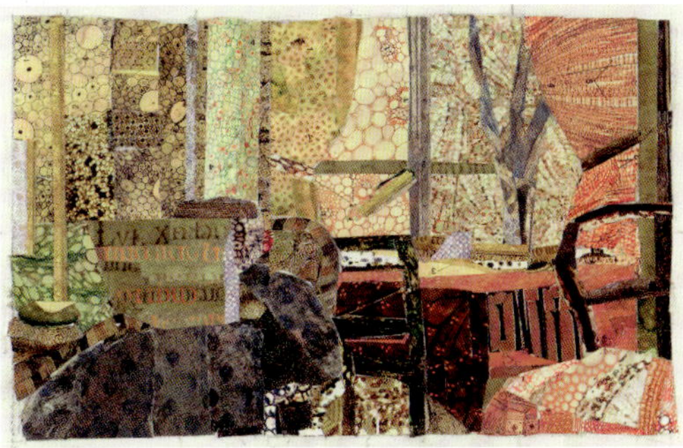

12. ***After Vuillard/Lisant,*** 2007
Collage
7 x 11 inches

13. ***Madonna and Child,*** 2007
Collage
18 x 13 inches

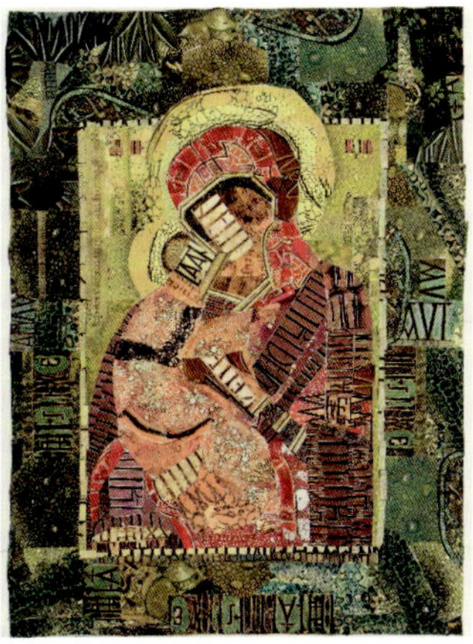

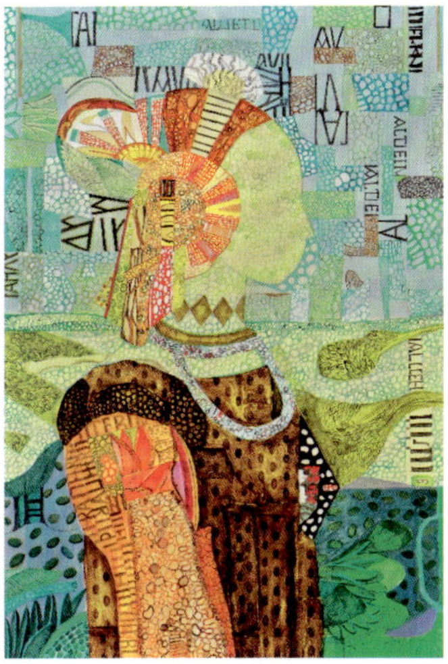

14. ***Ritratto I,*** 2007
Acrylic on board
36 x 24 inches

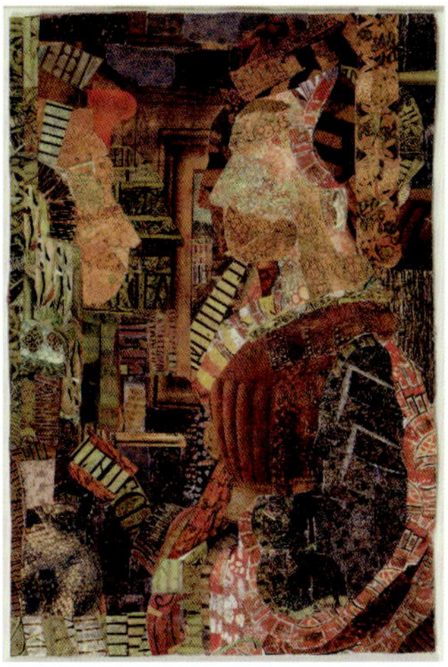

15. ***At the Window,*** 2008
Collage
20 x 13 inches

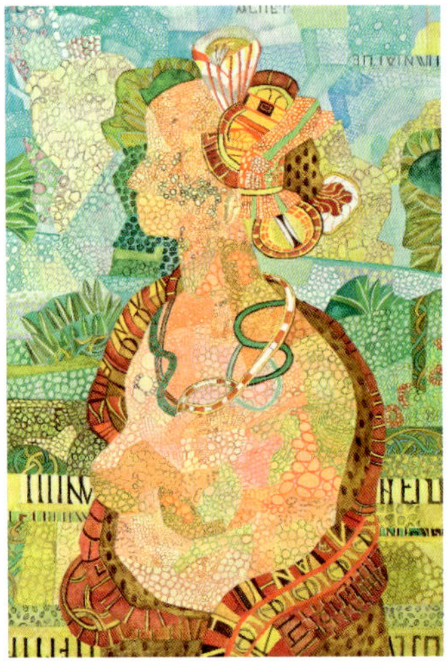

16. ***Cleopatra,*** 2008
Acrylic on board
36 x 24 inches

17. ***Donna,*** 2008
Collage
20 x 14 inches

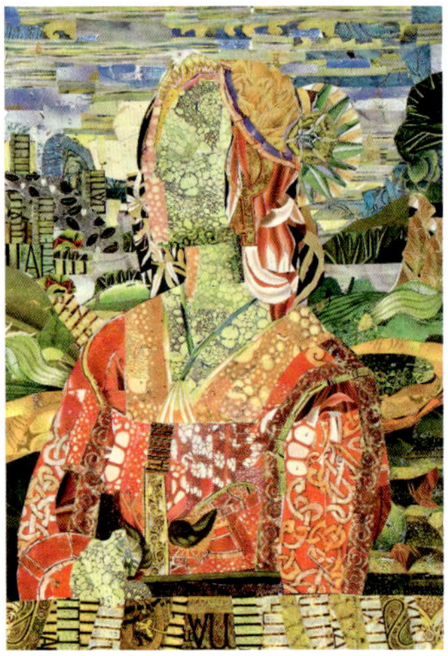

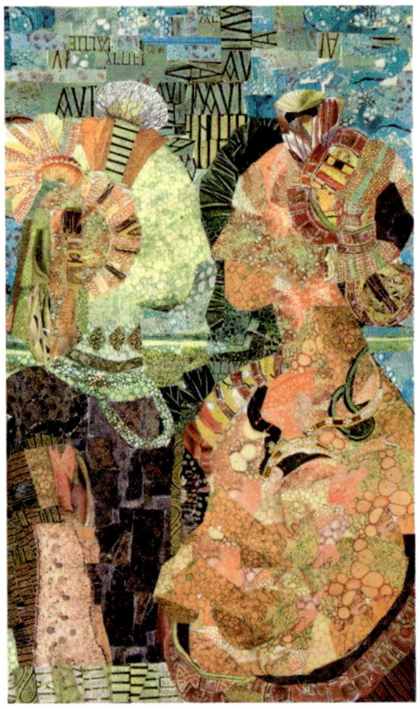

18. ***Incontriamo,*** 2008
Collage
24 x 14 inches

19. ***Ritratto V,*** 2008
Acrylic on board
36 x 24 inches

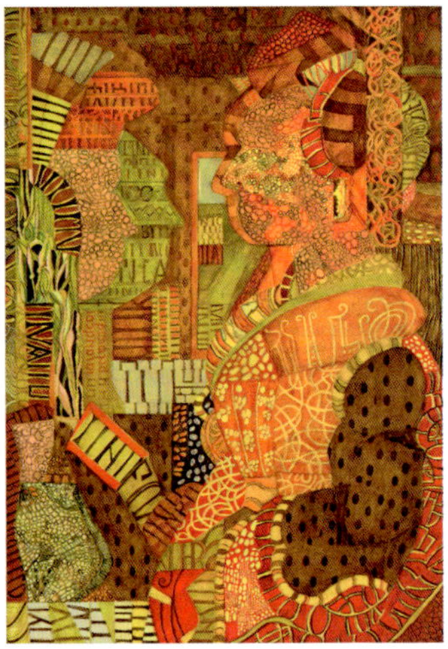

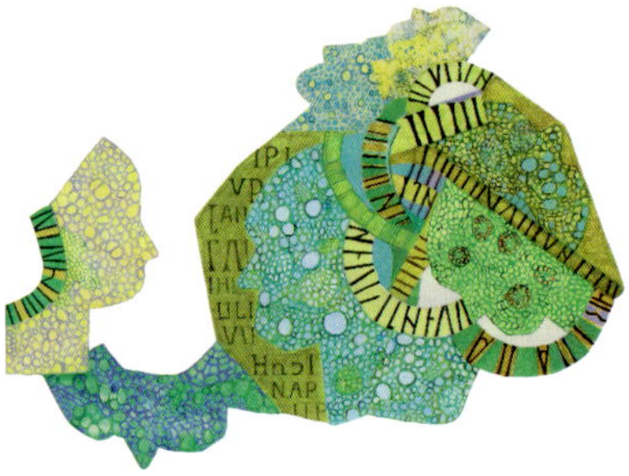

20. ***Tipsy II,*** 2008
Acrylic and collage on board
18 x 22 inches

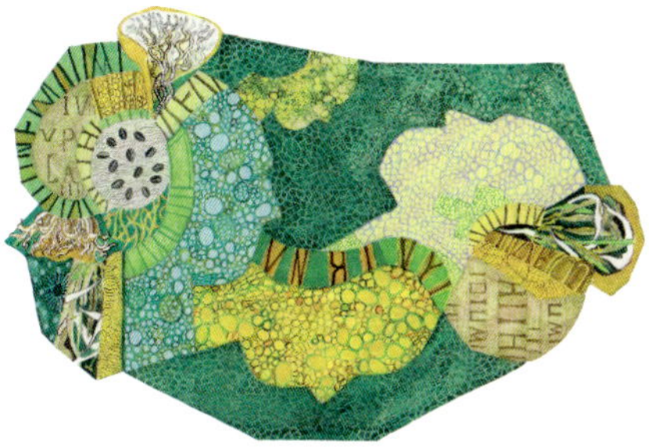

21. ***Tipsy III,*** 2008
Acrylic and collage on board
18 x 24 inches

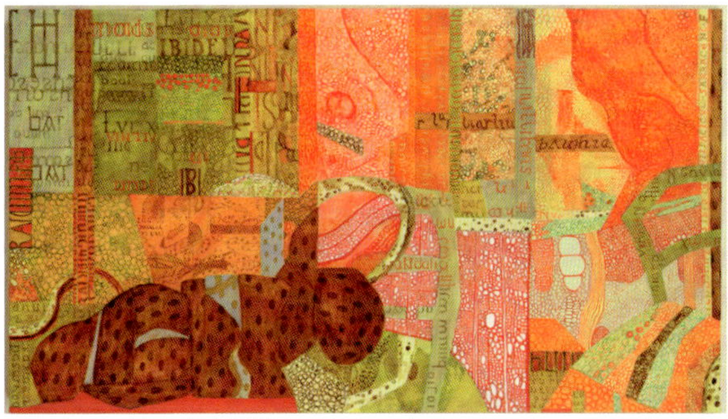

22. ***Lisant IV,*** 2009
Acrylic on canvas
38 x 68 inches

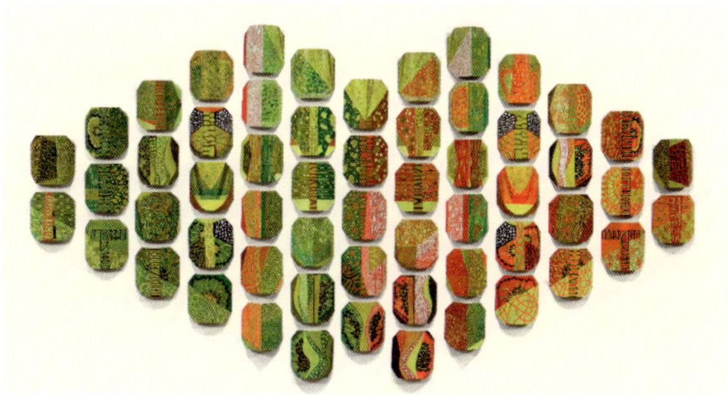

23. ***Djellaba,*** 2010
Fifty-seven-piece installation;
acrylic on metal
94 x 194 x 3 inches

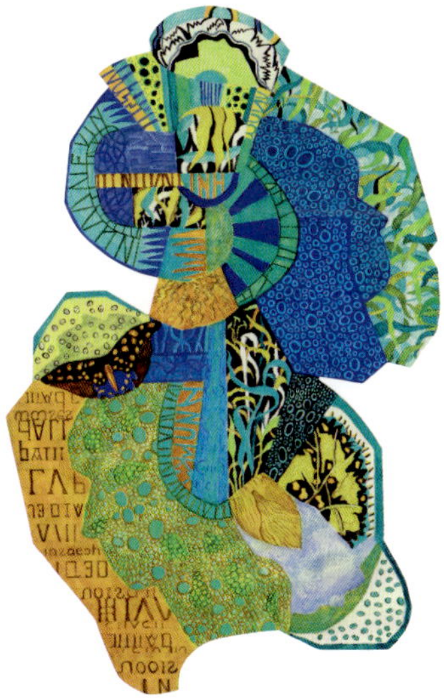

24. ***Duo,*** 2010
Acrylic and oil on board
45 x 29 inches

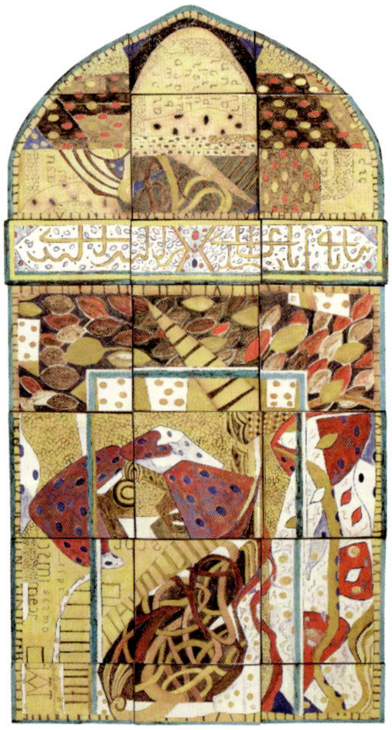

25. ***Portal,*** 2010
Twenty-one ceramic *maiolica* tiles
65 x 34 inches

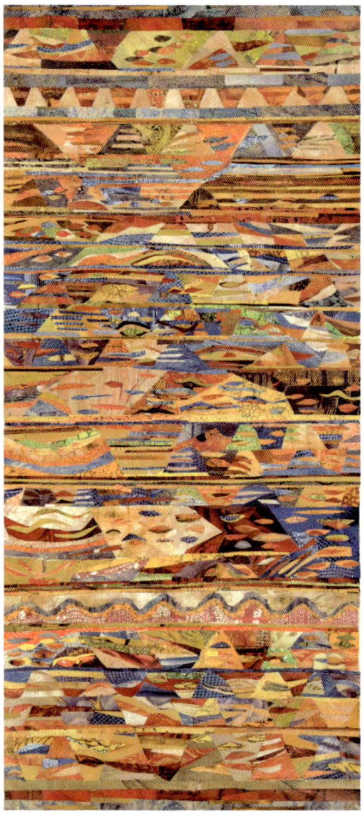

26. ***Tit 'n-teskourt,*** 2010
Collage (color Xerox)
35.5 x 15.5 inches

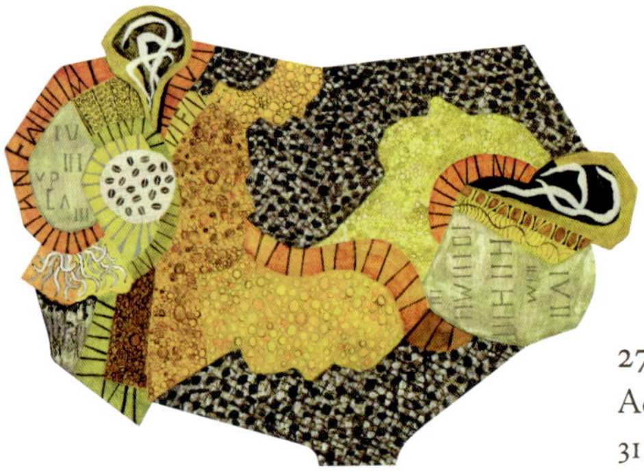

27. ***Trio IV,*** 2010
Acrylic and oil on board
31 x 44 inches

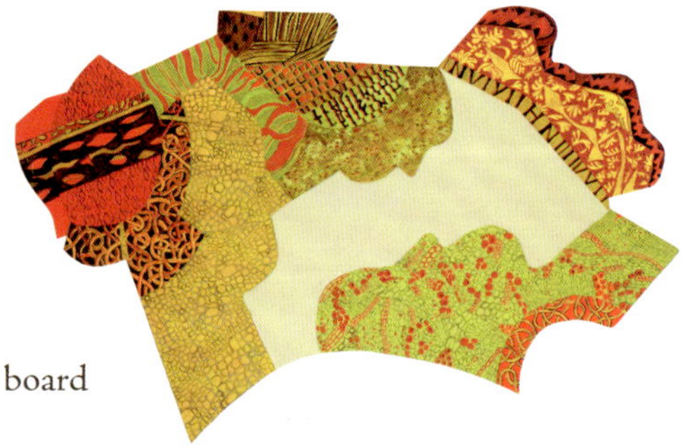

28. ***Trio V,*** 2010
Acrylic and oil on board
30 x 46 inches